MACMILLAN MAS

CW01022813

GENERAL EDITOR: JAMES GIBSON

Published

JANE AUSTEN	*Emma* Norman Page
	Persuasion Judy Simons
	Sense and Sensibility Judy Simons
	Pride and Prejudice Raymond Wilson
	Mansfield Park Richard Wirdnam
SAMUEL BECKETT	*Waiting for Godot* Jennifer Birkett
WILLIAM BLAKE	*Songs of Innocence* and *Songs of Experience* Alan Tomlinson
ROBERT BOLT	*A Man for All Seasons* Leonard Smith
CHARLOTTE BRONTË	*Jane Eyre* Robert Miles
EMILY BRONTË	*Wuthering Heights* Hilda D. Spear
GEOFFREY CHAUCER	*The Miller's Tale* Michael Alexander
	The Pardoner's Tale Geoffrey Lester
	The Wife of Bath's Tale Nicholas Marsh
	The Knight's Tale Anne Samson
	The Prologue to the Canterbury Tales Nigel Thomas and Richard Swan
JOSEPH CONRAD	*The Secret Agent* Andrew Mayne
CHARLES DICKENS	*Bleak House* Dennis Butts
	Great Expectations Dennis Butts
	Hard Times Norman Page
GEORGE ELIOT	*Middlemarch* Graham Handley
	Silas Marner Graham Handley
	The Mill on the Floss Helen Wheeler
T. S. ELIOT	*Murder in the Cathedral* Paul Lapworth
	Selected Poems Andrew Swarbrick
HENRY FIELDING	*Joseph Andrews* Trevor Johnson
E. M. FORSTER	*Howards End* Ian Milligan
	A Passage to India Hilda D. Spear
WILLIAM GOLDING	*The Spire* Rosemary Sumner
	Lord of the Flies Raymond Wilson
OLIVER GOLDSMITH	*She Stoops to Conquer* Paul Ranger
THOMAS HARDY	*The Mayor of Casterbridge* Ray Evans
	Tess of the d'Urbervilles James Gibson
	Far from the Madding Crowd Colin Temblett-Wood
GERARD MANLEY HOPKINS	*Selected Poems* R. J. C. Watt
JOHN KEATS	*Selected Poems* John Garrett
BEN JONSON	*Volpone* Michael Stout
PHILIP LARKIN	*The Whitsun Weddings* and *The Less Deceived* Andrew Swarbrick
D. H. LAWRENCE	*Sons and Lovers* R. P. Draper
HARPER LEE	*To Kill a Mockingbird* Jean Armstrong
LAURIE LEE	*Cider with Rosie* Brian Tarbitt

MACMILLAN MASTER GUIDES

CHRISTOPHER MARLOWE	*Doctor Faustus* David A. Male
THE METAPHYSICAL POETS	Joan van Emden
THOMAS MIDDLETON and WILLIAM ROWLEY	*The Changeling* Tony Bromham
ARTHUR MILLER	*The Crucible* Leonard Smith *Death of a Salesman* Peter Spalding
GEORGE ORWELL	*Animal Farm* Jean Armstrong
WILLIAM SHAKESPEARE	*Richard II* Charles Barber *Hamlet* Jean Brooks *Othello* Tony Bromham *King Lear* Francis Casey *Henry V* Peter Davison *The Winter's Tale* Diana Devlin *Julius Caesar* David Elloway *Macbeth* David Elloway *The Merchant of Venice* A. M. Kinghorn *Measure for Measure* Mark Lilly *Henry IV Part I* Helen Morris *A Midsummer Night's Dream* Kenneth Pickering *Romeo and Juliet* Helen Morris *The Tempest* Kenneth Pickering *Coriolanus* Gordon Williams *Antony and Cleopatra* Martin Wine
GEORGE BERNARD SHAW	*St Joan* Leonée Ormond
RICHARD SHERIDAN	*The School for Scandal* Paul Ranger *The Rivals* Jeremy Rowe
ALFRED TENNYSON	*In Memoriam* Richard Gill
ANTHONY TROLLOPE	*Barchester Towers* K. M. Newton
JOHN WEBSTER	*The White Devil* and *The Duchess of Malfi* David A. Male
VIRGINIA WOOLF	*To the Lighthouse* John Mepham *Mrs Dalloway* Julian Pattison
WILLIAM WORDSWORTH	*The Prelude Books I and II* Helen Wheeler

Forthcoming

JOHN BUNYAN	*The Pilgrim's Progress* Beatrice Batson
RUDYARD KIPLING	*Kim* Leonée Ormond
JOHN MILTON	*Comus* Tom Healy
WILLIAM SHAKESPEARE	*As You Like It* Kiernan Ryan
W. B. YEATS	*Selected Poems* Stan Smith

MACMILLAN MASTER GUIDES

CIDER WITH ROSIE

BY LAURIE LEE

BRIAN TARBITT

M

**MACMILLAN
EDUCATION**

Printed in Hong Kong

British Library Catologuing in Publication Data
Tarbitt, Brian
Cider with Rosie by Laurie Lee.—(Macmillan
master guides).
1. Lee, Laurie. Cider with Rosie
I. Title II. Lee, Laurie. Cider with Rosie
942.4′17083′0924   PR6023.E
ISBN 0–333–44276–8 Pbk
ISBN 0–333–44277–6 Pbk export

CONTENTS

GENERAL EDITOR'S PREFACE

The aim of the Macmillan Master Guides is to help you to appreciate the book you are studying by providing information about it and by suggesting ways of reading and thinking about it which will lead to a fuller understanding. The section on the writer's life and background has been designed to illustrate those aspects of the writer's life which have influenced the work, and to place it in its personal and literary context. The summaries and critical commentary are of special importance in that each brief summary of the action is followed by an examination of the significant critical points. The space which might have been given to repetitive explanatory notes has been devoted to a detailed analysis of the kind of passage which might confront you in an examination. Literary criticism is concerned with both the broader aspects of the work being studied and with its detail. The ideas which meet us in reading a great work of literature, and their relevance to us today, are an essential part of our study, and our Guides look at the thought of their subject in some detail. But just as essential is the craft with which the writer has constructed his work of art, and this may be considered under several technical headings – characterisation, language, style and stagecraft, for example.

The authors of these Guides are all teachers and writers of wide experience, and they have chosen to write about books they admire and know well in the belief that they can communicate their admiration to you. But you yourself must read and know intimately the book you are studying. No one can do that for you. You should see this book as a lamp-post. Use it to shed light, not to lean against. If you know your text and know what it is saying about life, and how it says it, then you will enjoy it, and there is no better way of passing an examination in literature.

JAMES GIBSON

ACKNOWLEDGEMENTS

All page references in this book refer to the edition of *Cider with Rosie* published by Penguin Books Ltd, Harmondsworth, Middlesex, England.

B.T.B.

The author and publishers wish to thank the following who have kindly given permission for the use of copyright material. Chatto & Windus Ltd. and The Hogarth Press Ltd. for extracts from *Cider With Rosie* by Laurie Lee, 1959, The Hogarth Press.

Every effort has been made to trace all the copyright holders but if any have been inadvertently overlooked the publishers will be pleased to make the necessary arrangements at the first opportunity.

Cover illustration: a detail from *Farms near Auvers* by Vincent Van Gogh. Photograph © Tate Gallery Publications.

1 LAURIE LEE:
AN INTRODUCTION

It is perhaps typical of Lee's individuality and 'otherness' that in *Cider with Rosie*, an autobiography, he does not actually tell us when he was born. In fact, the date was 26 June 1914, just a few short weeks before the outbreak of the First World War, which was almost at an end when that book opened. The place of his birth was Stroud, a small Gloucestershire town. Lee's was a large family, with three half-sisters, two half-brothers (one of whom, however, lived with his grandmother) and two full brothers. His father left his mother when Laurie was very young (though with an even younger brother), necessitating the move of the family to the valley village of Slad and the cottage which was to be his home until he left to make his remarkable journey to Spain.

This journey he recounted years later in *As I Walked Out One Midsummer Morning*. It took him – all on foot – from his home down to the south coast of England, and then up to London; after several months spent laying bricks he again took to his feet, spent four pounds on a ticket to Vigo, in northern Spain, and from there walked the length of the country, taking in some of the great towns and cities but also treading the virtually unknown tracks of that fascinating country, ending on what is now the Costa del Sol. (This journey, undertaken by a young boy of nineteen to twenty, entirely alone, without even a smattering of Spanish when he set out, without money, and in a country visited by very few Britons, was an astonishing venture.)

After being evacuated from Spain by the Royal Navy, because of the increasing danger to British citizens created by the onset of the Spanish Civil War, he returned briefly to England. But his identification with Spain and its tragic problems soon compelled him to go back again. The Civil War over, he then spent further time tramping the Mediterranean area. For financial support he played the fiddle on the streets – a skill he alludes to in *Cider with Rosie* and develops in *As I Walked Out One Midsummer Morning*.

But it was his other great talent, writing, which was to sustain him from that time onwards. By the end of *Cider with Rosie* he had begun 'to make up poems from intense abstraction . . . imagination scarcely faltering once, rhythm hardly skipping a beat'. To a succession of wartime and post-war jobs with official Film Units, and a spell as Publications Editor with the Ministry of Information, was added his first published book of poems, *The Sun My Monument* (1944) followed by *The Bloom of Candles* (1947) and *My Many-Coated Man* (1955). As well as these volumes he produced prose works and drama: *Land at War* (1945); *A Film in Cyprus* (1947, jointly with Frank Keene); *The Voyage of Magellan* (1948); and *A Rose for Winter* (1955).

However, it was *Cider with Rosie* (1959) – published a year later in the USA as *Edge of Day* – which brought him to a much wider audience; *As I Walked Out One Midsummer Morning* (1969) and *I Can't Stay Long* (1975) have also been widely acclaimed, the British Broadcasting Corporation recently producing a splendid two-hour account of *As I Walked Out One Midsummer Morning*, with Lee himself reading voice-over extracts from the work. Among many prizes and awards gained by his writings are the W. H. Smith Award for Literature (for *Cider with Rosie*) and the Foyle Poetry Award (for *My Many-Coated Man*); his work has also been the 'special choice' of various book clubs and societies.

Lee married in 1950; his daughter is the subject of *The Firstborn* (1964). He was awarded the MBE in 1952 and now lives mainly in London, listing his recreations as 'indoor sports, music, travel'.

2 SECTION SUMMARIES

AND

CRITICAL COMMENTARY

SECTION 1   FIRST LIGHT

Summary

Young Laurie Lee, just three years old, is brought to his new home, a cottage in a Gloucestershire village which he is to share with his mother, brothers and sisters until he is almost twenty. The section is a ragbag of memories from his first year there: his terror on first arrival when he was alone for the first time in his life; his discovery of the teeming abundance of nature all around him; the arrival of a soldier who had deserted from the war; the end of the First World War, with its attendant wildness and celebrations.

Commentary

In reading and discussing *Cider with Rosie* we must constantly remind ourselves that what we are dealing with is not a novel but an autobiography. This will affect our approach in several ways. First, we will not be looking for the type of structured plot which a novel contains, with its 'beginning, middle and end' (however much those may be tampered with). We may well expect to see, however, a narrative framework of sorts, determined by the normal passage of time; this expectation will be realised, rather loosely at times, in *Cider with Rosie*. Secondly, we must not look for the selection of detail which, in a novel, is largely the work of the author's imagination. In *Cider with Rosie* the detail is real, and selected not by imagination but by memory. No one has ever satisfactorily explained why we remember some incidents and forget others, nor will the subect be discussed here: Laurie Lee's memories of his early years seem at times logical, but just as often random. Third is the question of characterisation. A novelist 'makes' characters, gives them the qualities he wishes, allows his narrative to develop from the people he has created (or, in poorer novels, slots the characters into the story he has to tell). Laurie Lee, on the other hand, is describing real people – his mother, Marjorie, Dorothy and the rest; their roles, too, are 'historical', not imaginary. It is not for him to invent qualities or situations, though we must remember that we 'see' any character, whether real or imaginary, through our own eyes only; we know only that part of themselves which they let us see. Last is the importance which attaches to the writer himself in his book. Lee is telling his own life story (or part of it); he can not be other than the central figure in it, no matter how self-effacing he is, nor how often things happen to him rather than through him.

All this should be borne in mind in examining the opening section of the book. Its heading, 'First Light' is perhaps an indication of what the whole book is about – the gradual awakening of young Laurie into the dawn, the gradual opening of his eyes to Life, the gradual 'creation' (almost in the biblical sense) of this new human being. (It is worth noting that *Cider with Rosie* was called *Edge of Day* when first published in the United States of America.)

The first few pages are full of a bewildering abundance of images: images which are full of colour, light, vitality, wildness; images in which all five senses run free, almost riotously out of control. This kind of writing, which is very typical of Lee's style, will be looked at much more closely later, in the section on Technical Features. Notice here, however, that it is a style which requires the writer to fill every available word with a powerful evocation of one or more of the senses; what the poet John Keats called 'loading every rift with ore'. So in the third paragraph are such words as 'tropic heat', 'oozed', 'rank', 'sharp odours', 'nettles', 'snow-clouds', 'elder-blossom', 'showering', 'fumes', 'flakes', 'sweet', 'giddy suffocation' – and all of that in only two sentences.

It is particularly appropriate that Lee uses this style in the earliest sections of his book, because it serves to convey just how fresh and alive the world seemed – as it would to a three-year-old child in a new environment. Here Lee is projecting himself backwards in time, conjuring up a child's view of the world; not, of course, using a child's language, but beautifully re-creating a child's innocent perceptions of the world around him. The early part of the book is almost entirely written from the child's standpoint; but by way of contrast, notice such passages as the one on p.14, where he takes the child's experience (in this case of repeated visits to see 'well-prodded horrors') and, as an adult, shows how, in this way, the 'destroying force' becomes less terrifying because one is seeing it in reality, in the cat's 'grub-captured carcass', not imagining it in a nightmarish terror.

As in a novel, the writer of an autobiography has to build what may be called a 'frame of reference': that is, a setting, in the widest sense, for what he has to tell us. Notice how subtly Lee establishes this frame of reference; not for him the clumsy opening – 'I was born in 1914 in the village of . . . I had X brothers and Y sisters; my father had left my mother', and so on. Such details as these float into the section as gently as the elder-blossom already mentioned; yet a great deal of factual information is to be picked up in a careful reading.

As well as the teeming freshness of this first section there is, powerfully felt, the atmosphere of enormous love and warmth which exists in the cottage; it radiates from his mother and the older sisters, Marjorie and Dorothy, almost smothering him in its richness. He is constantly being picked up and cuddled, crammed full of berries, and 'mothered' like a doll. It is highly likely that the growing sexual awareness which is to be found throughout this book (and what is meant by 'sexual awareness' is simply the realisation that the female is other than the male – and not only physically) can be traced to these infant experiences, in which there is no father, and in which his brothers, significantly, are not mentioned at all.

SECTION 2   FIRST NAMES

Summary

Laurie's mother comes back home from her visit to his father; no explanation of their separation has as yet been offered. He describes the nights he spent as 'the baby' in his mother's bed; all too soon, however, and much to his disgust, his place was taken by his younger brother, Tony. This was a turning-point, for now he began to look beyond the house for his interest and adventures, to the yard and the village, with its legends and eccentrics (for who remembers the ordinary and the commonplace?). Most of the legends are gruesome or ghostly – tales of violent death, monstrous creatures, bizarre coincidence. Not so the 'characters', many of whom are endearing rather than frightening in their oddity, calling up amusement or compassion rather than terror.

It was 'from the age of five or so' that Laurie 'began to grow acquainted with these neighbours'. He gives a further marker for our frame of reference a little later in this section when he speaks of 'the long hot summer of 1921' (when he would be seven). The drought was followed by torrential rain, which regularly disrupted the life of the Lee family, usually in the middle of the night, by bringing the danger (or even the reality) of the flooding of their cottage.

Commentary

It is again worth looking at the heading of the section – in this case, 'First Names'. Laurie Lee was a poet first (and a very good one) before he started writing prose, and it is fairly certain that this heading was chosen with care. What does it suggest? First, a growing feeling of intimacy with his surroundings; to be on 'first name' terms with someone normally means that a friendship exists. Next, a growth in his powers of language, the great medium of communication which he obviously loves so much; he can now give names, gradually, to that multitude of objects which surrounds him. Finally, a growing sense of his 'otherness', his separateness from all other things; once someone, or something, has a name it marks them apart from all other things. A central feature of growing up (which is a central theme of this book, of course) is that one gradually goes through this process of separation, which normally reaches its final stage when one leaves the family home to start to lead one's own life and build the next generation.

In this section, then, one sees this process in a very early stage, on p.28, after he has been 'betrayed' by his mother, who now sleeps with young Tony: 'I grew a little tougher, a little colder, and turned my attention more towards the outside world, which by now was emerging visibly through the mist.' Before this, however, Lee has evoked a beautiful picture of the nights he spent in his mother's bed; all the comfort, the love, the longing, the one-ness, the warmth of that closest of all relationships is seen there; and though young Laurie is mortified when he must sleep in 'the boys' room', a very tight bond of emotion has been forged between him and his mother, seen almost every time he mentions her, but especially visible in the section called simply 'Mother'.

After his 'rejection' comes the discovery of the outside world of the village. Interestingly, he is at first aware of it through 'magic and fear'; in other words it is the logical extension of the 'daylight uneasiness' and night-time terrors of the cottage, peopled by 'Old Men' and other bogeys of his (or his sisters') imagination. In considering the tales he now re-tells, or the 'characters' he recalls, it should perhaps be remembered that the England of his early childhood was a very different place from what it is today, especially in matters of communication. A village in a Gloucestershire valley was an isolated place indeed, almost unchanged over many centuries; those amenities – especially radio and television – which today can put even the remotest communities in instant touch with the wider world were dreams for a distant future. The people made their own entertainment, their stories carried down by word of mouth over endless generations. Small wonder that superstition, exaggeration and wild legend all flourished, as they do in every 'primitive' settlement; and that the young Laurie's imagination was constantly awakened by the tales that were so much a part of the family's lamplit, fireside conversation.

Jones's goat is perhaps the best illustration of the 'magic and fear' of the outside world, for it has two feet in the world of reality and two feet in that other world of myth and superstition. A real goat it certainly is, though possibly some of its dimensions and powers have been magnified by the memory. But it is the other qualities that are much more interesting, those which stretch back in time to our most primitive origins. The goat is the supreme symbol of male sexuality and evil, in close combination: in both Roman and Greek mythologies we find goats, or half-men, half-goats, or gods disguised as goats; a favourite guise of the Devil in Christian literature is the goat; goats abound in Satanism; and so on.

Lee, of course, treats the matter of Jones's goat with a good deal more humour than is perhaps suggested above, yet the reactions of the girls and the women, the combination of terror and fascination, the hysteria, are very real. This combination of feelings is particularly characteristic of girls' sexuality – as we see later in this section in a very different passage concerning Percy-from-Painswick, whose words would 'befuddle the girls and set them shrieking with *pleasure and shock*'; they would 'run screaming down over the bank, red-faced, excited, incredulous, hiding in bushes to exclaim to each other was it possible what Percy just said?' Throughout the book Lee's approach is totally honest. He makes no attempt to conceal the 'horrors' of his young life, and he likewise constantly presents sex for what it is – one of the most powerful and basic of all our natural human drives, riddled with myth and superstition, but with a comical side that perhaps only the adult eye can see. So it is in this section.

Finally, *Cider with Rosie* is a book full of references and allusions. Sometimes these are literary – a word or phrase from Shakespeare, or an echo of Dylan Thomas. The flood at this section's end seems very reminiscent of the great Flood in the Bible, with its panic of a drowning world. What is the evidence? There is little, perhaps, other

than the way the language suddenly seems full of 'religious' turns of
phrase not typical of the rest of the book: 'Hell in Heaven!'; 'Jesus
have mercy on us!'; 'Sweet saints above!'; 'lamentations reached
elegiac proportions'; 'Gods', 'Saints', 'Fates', 'the eternal drain'; plus
the fact that in 'First Light' there are powerful suggestions of the
biblical Creation, as already mentioned. The reader should not infer
that there is any great significance in this, but should be aware that
such references come naturally to Lee's pen, preoccupied as it is in
these sections with his earliest, deepest and possibly most primitive
memories.

SECTION 3   VILLAGE SCHOOL

Summary

The village is now presented to us in a slightly wider geographical
setting; its life, both plant and animal, is described briefly; then the
way of life of the inhabitants; finally the buildings, leading to the
main subject of this section, the village school. Here for the first time
Laurie encounters children outside his own family. His two years in
the Infant School, with at first his warm, young, female teacher, are
his last days of innocence. Once in the 'Big Room' he has to learn the
selfish skills necessary for survival. Two of his brothers now appear:
Jack, the very bright and studious one, and Tony, defiant and
obstinate.

The head teacher, 'Crabby', is something of a tyrant, so much so
that eventually there is a rebellion by 'Spadge' Hopkins who, in a
memorable scene, lifts her up and sits her on top of a cupboard. Soon
afterwards she resigns. Miss Wardley, the new teacher from Birming-
ham, has a rather more civilised view of education. Laurie eventually wins her approval by writing essays about otters, even though
he is largely inventing the material. When the time comes for him to
leave school, he realises that he has relished at least some of his time
there for the vitality he found, for the comradeship he developed with
other boys, and perhaps even for some of the rote learning of basic
matters that was drilled into him. The section ends with a rather
philosophical page or two, examined more closely in the commentary.

Commentary

Again, the emerging pattern of the book is becoming clearer: as the
years pass, so the horizon broadens. Not only do we have a

wide-angle view of the village but also the author's 'voice' (see the reference to a passage from p.14 in the commentary on 'First Light') is becoming increasingly the voice of the adult looking back at childhood. This is especially noticeable in the final two pages of the section, which will be examined later.

Laurie's response to female company early in this section is again unmistakeable: 'those two blonde girls, already puppyishly pretty, whose names and bodies were to distract and haunt me for the next fifteen years of my life'; 'counting beads which our young teacher played like a harp, leaning her bosom against our faces'; 'to suggest I might watch her getting dressed in the morning seemed to me both outrageous and wonderful.' There are two important landmarks in this section, the first a milestone passed, the second a gateway reached. The first, the move from the Infant School to the 'Big Room', is a move into a world 'both adult and tough'; the carefree, self-indulgent world of infancy has gone for good; he can no longer count on the protective shell of family or infant teacher to shield him from the appalling things which human beings do to each other. He must learn to be independent, to fend for himself. The second, at the very end of the section, is the point at which he has reached the gate into the outside world; his schooldays are over, the world awaits. (We do not, in fact, pass through that gate in the rest of the book, and so this section marks the end of the first, larger part of *Cider with Rosie*.)

'Village School' is much more concerned with the writer's own development than the previous sections. He is having to come to terms with a wider social world than his close family; to learn the social conventions (such as not hitting Vera over the head with a stick!); to cope with the bullies and the bullied; to accept that others, too, have their right to a place in the world. The kind of formal education current at the time, the 1920s, was clearly not much to Lee's taste, and in that sense he learned little more than the elementary facts which were 'enough to get by with'. But there were more positive and long-lasting qualities that he took from his school life: his view of humanity is widened – he has been given his 'first amazed vision of any world outside the womanly warmth of [his] family'; he has learned tolerance – 'our inborn hatred for freaks and outcasts was tempered by meeting them daily'; he has learned that real worth and value in a human being do not necessarily go hand in hand with great academic ability; and he has acquired perhaps the most noble of all human feelings, compassion.

In this section also is witnessed the growing up of a boy for whom the outdoors is the natural element. School, especially in summer-time, could be a torment to him in its irrelevance. One of the few things he finds easy, significantly enough, is the writing of poetry; and he also writes successful essays about the lives of otters; though he claims never to have seen one, surely his instinctive oneness with the life of the countryside made him seem convincing! We must beware, however, of presenting too priggish a picture of young Laurie; many episodes in this section show him to be just as capable as any other boy of telling 'fibs', of truanting, of playing tricks, telling jokes, grumbling about work to be done, being curious about girls, and so on. Clearly the other boys in the school saw him as no different from themselves (unlike his clever brother, Jack); he is part of the unbreakable chain which boys can form themselves into; they are, in his words, 'indivisibly male'.

And so to the final pages of the section. As the young Laurie has grown in 'Village School' (which does, after all, span ten years) so the tone of the writing has become more sober; the world has become a harsher place than it was when the cottage garden was its outer limit. From 'So our school work was done' (p.57) he grows philosophical; the mood is compassionate. He is drawn in sympathy to Rosso, the poor gipsy child, 'with nothing but mud and puddles to sit in and the sour banks to scavenge for food', while he himself goes home to his 'cabbage dinner'. The world may condemn Nick and Edna, innocent offspring of an incestuous relationship, but not Laurie Lee, nor the other children, to whom Nick and Edna were just two children, like any others. Of course, like all 'primitives', the school children could be merciless and cruel. But at the same time Laurie Lee clearly has a very deep sense of, and feeling for, the sufferings of humanity. The section ends, appropriately enough, on a note of sadness – the teacher who knew they would never go back to see her; nostalgia for the days gone by – but impatience, too, for the life that lay ahead, through the gateway.

SECTION 4   THE KITCHEN

Summary

After an opening indication of how strong the influence of his home was, Lee begins a series of more detailed descriptions, beginning with his father. We learn that Laurie's mother had been first his house-keeper, then his second wife, taking over five children and then producing four more of her own, one of whom died. The father, 'a natural fixer' and more than a little irresponsible, left his wife and the eight children when Laurie was three. There follow character sketches of the children – Marjorie, Dorothy and Phyllis, Laurie's half-sisters, of whom he was enormously fond; his half-brother, Harold; and his full brothers, Jack and Tony. Each of them was very special to the writer. Turning to their cottage in the village, Lee provides a clearer and more total picture of its interior, finally focusing on the kitchen. The rest of the section is taken up with an account of a typical day in the Lee household, from getting up to going to bed.

Commentary

Whereas the three previous sections in the book have been more or less chronological, moving from Laurie's first memory of the cottage, aged three, to his leaving school, this section has comparatively little reference to time, but rather to place; it is a whole series of memories boiled down into an essence, as if a considerable span of time has become a mere, typical day. And whereas the author's 'voice' in the previous sections has been mostly the voice of the child he was, with a child's naivety and insights, here he writes almost entirely as the adult, looking back to his childhood.

This difference is immediately apparent: the young Laurie was so caught up in all that was happening around him, the teeming life, the hosts of new experiences, that he was unable to stand back and look at it all objectively; he almost literally could not see the wood for the trees. This section, however, begins with several more distanced character sketches of his father, his brothers and sisters. It is not easy to be sure of Lee's tone in writing of his father, but there seems more than a little contempt, even bitterness, in it: a smooth talker who was in the war but avoided the fighting; whose first wife died young after giving birth to eight children; who recklessly fathered another four – on nineteen shillings a week; and who finally left them all, and Laurie's mother, as 'a sprawling, cumbersome, countrified brood too incongruous to carry with him'. Small wonder that Laurie 'scarcely missed him'.

When it comes to his half-sisters, however, there is no doubt whatever about the enormous love he felt for them as a child, and still feels in writing his book. These girls will be looked at more closely in a later section of this book; suffice it to say at this stage that each sketch is a model of its kind, concerned not so much with simple physical description as with capturing the essence and spirit of each girl; the outward trappings and form matter little – the real person is what is inside, and underneath. His brothers receive rather less attention at this point, no doubt because the girls, being the oldest, had so much more of the looking-after of the boys to do – and Laurie, it must be remembered, was the youngest of all, except for Tony.

The new objectivity in the writing is also seen when Lee turns to the cottage; though he indicates how many floors it had, how many rooms, who slept where, and so forth, there is an increasing feeling that the cottage is itself another character in his life. His memories of it are inseparable from his memories of his family in those childhood days, and the warmth of his feelings seeps into the very stone. (It was, after all, far more than just a house from the very beginning; even in 'First Light' it became an extension of the overflowing garden, 'its dim interior seemed entirely possessed by the world outside – a still green pool flooding with honeyed tides of summer').

Why is this section entitled 'The Kitchen'? The answer surely is clear, though perhaps with a different emphasis from the previous sections: in looking back to all those vivid days with an overwhelming warmth and nostalgia, Lee finds the focal point of it all is the kitchen; when thinking of and 'seeing' his family, they are frequently in the setting of the kitchen, the core of their home. It was warm, it was intimate, it was a vital heart – a symbol of all that his childhood meant to him. The family life he recalls was a ritual: chaotic and disordered, but nevertheless a ritual; the kitchen was as central to that ritual as the altar is to a Christian church.

For the rest of the section Lee describes a day's activities. Jack, with whom he sleeps, is sharp from the very moment of waking (and to the moment of falling asleep, as we see at the end of the section); then it is down to the kitchen for a haphazard breakfast. The girls by now all have jobs, as has Harold, and snatch a hurried bite; the younger boys are either off to school or out to roam the countryside, but it is always to the twin havens of mother and kitchen that they return: 'every stone in the path as I ran down home shook my bones with arriving joy'.

The ritual of the evening is more orderly, but just as rich in its variety: the candles are lit and set out, 'each in its proper order' (ritual again); then the iron lamp is lit; Laurie has his violin practice, which binds him even closer to his appreciative mother, while Jack engages in an intellectual activity and Tony occupies his solitary world. Great importance in the kitchen is attached to the fire, another very primitive, almost tribal, symbol of security and bonding. The girls return from work, the ritualistic pattern of the evening settles down; each works at a private activity – drawing, sewing, cutting up newspapers for a scrapbook – and yet they are welded in an unbreakable family unit; they are alone yet together; they are eight yet they are one. In Lee's mind as he looks back on this, that other 'character' – the kitchen – is the symbol of it all.

SECTION 5   GRANNIES IN THE WAINSCOT

Summary

Lee paints a further picture of the family cottage. It is in fact part of a larger building, in the shape of a letter 'T'; the Lee family occupy the downstroke, with the two floors of the crosspiece being two further homes, lived in by two very old women, Granny Trill and Granny Wallon (Granny being a courtesy title, not an indication of relationship). These two women live in an obsessive hatred of each other; they never speak to each other, nor do they refer to each other by name, yet each is fully aware of everything the other does.

Their life-styles are very different. Granny Wallon, who lives downstairs, spends the whole year, it seems, in making wines. She constantly scours the countryside around for almost any kind of vegetation – leaves, flowers, vegetables -- to bring home in great armfuls for fermentation. Her house, rather like the Lees' own, is a riot of foliage, colour and smell.

Granny Trill, on the other hand, is a much more private kind of woman, who can sit motionless for hours on end. She has had a very strange, even tragic, history. Her mother died when she was only five, after which young Alice and her father lived a seemingly wild, gipsy-like existence in the woods for ten years, until her father was killed in a gruesome accident, skewered to the ground by the branch of a falling tree. Unable to move it, she sat with her father for a whole twenty-four hours until he died. After that she was brought into the 'civilised' world of the Squire and the village, married to a gardener, and outlived him by many years.

The Lee children are regular and welcome visitors to both grannies, who are each glad of the chance to speak ill of the other. So the feud goes on over many years until Granny Trill has a fall, takes to her bed and dies. The big funeral (for the old lady was a 'landmark' in the village) is disturbed by Granny Wallon insisting that she was the older, not Granny Trill, as her coffin-plate indicates. Within a fortnight Granny Wallon, her last great task of outliving Granny Trill accomplished, dies too.

Commentary

If the preceding sections have shown that one of the noticeable factors in growing up is an increasing perception of space, a widening of one's sense of place (the cottage widens to the garden, to the village, to the valley, to a bird's-eye view of the whole) this section deals with the development of the other great imponderable – a sense of Time. The matter must be kept in proportion, however, for the section is first and foremost a superb portrait of two old ladies, memorable figures from Laurie's childhood, with whom he had the kind of relationship which often develops between people at the extremes of the human life-span. Nevertheless, through the fascination the Grannies have for him, Lee's simple awareness of Time and its passing is developed a stage or two further. Three relevant episodes will show this clearly.

The first is when we are introduced to Granny Trill (p.82). We are told she 'had an original sense of time which seemed to obey some vestigial pattern'. Now although this oddity of hers (getting up at 4a.m., eating at regular but unusual hours, and going to bed at 5p.m.) strikes young Laurie as 'monstrous', 'upsetting the roots of order', its unusualness causes him to ponder the question of time. He concludes: 'Granny Trill's time was for God, or the birds, and although she had a clock she kept it simply for the tick, its hands having dropped off years ago.' This last detail, though clearly comic at first, is of deep significance: Granny Trill's life, or the life of any individual, or the whole of recorded and unrecorded history, is made up of ticks; and whether a particular tick is identified as being 'four twenty-two and ten seconds precisely' does not really matter very much. The tick – the moving on of time, which never moves back – is all.

The second passage (pp.86–7) concerns the great beech tree which 'filled at least half the sky' in front of Granny Trill's end of the cottage. Laurie had just been listening to Granny's tales of her wedding, at the age of sixteen ('the age of our sister Dorothy') trying to equate the notion of a beautiful wild young girl with the aged, skinny figure in front of him, when she told him that her father had planted that beech. Now Laurie had another question of time to cope with. This vast tree, 'a city for owls and squirrels' with its main branches, its alleys, its shaded ways, was (it seemed to him) 'as old as the earth'. Yet Granny Trill's father had put the seed into the earth from which this huge living thing had sprung. Add Granny Trill's age to what Laurie now thinks her father's age must have been 'and you were back at the beginning of the world'. Through such experiences grew his understanding of time.

Finally there is the beautiful simile when Granny Trill dies (p.92). 'Like a delicate pale bubble, blown a little higher and further than the other girls of her generation, she had floated just long enough for us to catch sight of her, had hovered for an instant before our eyes; and then had popped suddenly, and disappeared for ever'. Here can be seen the full development in Lee of a perception of the nature of time, and in two ways. First, there is the realisation that a life – even as long a life as Granny Trill's ninety-five years – when set against the great backcloth of time is merely a bubble, flimsy, fragile and short-lasting. (There is a similar, equally beautiful simile in Anglo-Saxon literature in which life is compared to a sparrow's swift flight through a great hall, lit up at night. It comes out of the darkness, is visible for a fleeting second, and then disappears into the darkness again.) Granny Trill leaves 'nothing on the air but a faint-drying image and the tiniest cloud of snuff.' Secondly, there is the realisation that time in our human history is an endless repetion of overlapping lives. The very old Granny Trill and the very young Laurie Lee touched only briefly, but his own life and understanding have been enriched and deepened by the contact.

SECTION 6   PUBLIC DEATH, PRIVATE MURDER

Summary

This is a section with several separate narratives. First is the story of how a boy called Vincent, who had left the village years before, returns unexpectedly one winter evening as a prosperous young man from New Zealand. He brags of his wealth in the local bar, humiliating old and young for their failure to get up and go. On his way home he is set upon by local youths, who beat him to death. Though every villager knows the culprits, they all keep silence and the crime remains unsolved. Then comes the sad suicide of Miss Flynn, who drowns herself in the pond. She is a woman with a mysterious background, always spoken of in whispers, uncompleted sentences, or half-explained insinuations. Her death deeply impressed itself on Lee's imagination. Much superstition attached itself to Fred Bates, the milk-boy who discovered her body, for the very next day he saw a man crushed to death by a wagon.

After an interlude in which he adds more about the village and its attitudes, and remembers the deaths of many of the old villagers, Lee returns to his anecdotes, writing about two old couples. The first of these, Mr and Mrs Davies, were a typical pair, living in comparative poverty, who had quite simply come to the end of their days. It is probably a visit to the dying man which Laurie made with his mother which created a deep impression on his mind. The final tale is perhaps the saddest episode in the whole book. Joseph and Hannah Brown, an old, dignified couple, still totally wrapped up in each other, take ill. The authorities insist on putting them in a workhouse, since they cannot look after themselves. There, they are separated; within a week, both are dead.

Commentary

Four stories are told in this brief section, and each shows Lee's supreme skill as a storyteller. With only a few strokes he paints the most vivid of pictures, and fills them with powerful emotion. However, the question of Lee as a narrator will be dealt with later in this book and so will not be developed here.

The first story, of the brutal murder of the returning villager, poses an interesting (though unasked) question. What were Lee's own feelings about it? He appears to take no moral stance, neither condemning nor condoning the action (cowardly or envious?) of the gang who murdered Vincent. He states simply that the young men continued to live in the village, untainted. But perhaps there are two sentences in this section which go some way towards providing an explanation: 'They belonged to the village and the village looked after them' (p.98); 'There was also a frank and unfearful attitude to death, and an acceptance of violence as a kind of ritual which no one accused or pardoned.' (P.105). Here is illustrated the very tight nature of the village community. The gang of youths would never have done to a stranger what they did to Vincent. In their eyes, however, he had done the unforgiveable: he had been of the village but, having made good in the wider world, had returned to taunt them, to show his contempt for the village, for them, and all that both represented.

The closely knit aspect of the village life is a very noticeable feature of this section. Lee explains it best on pp.104–5, writing of the village's ancient past: 'since the Stone Age'; it is as if everything that had happened in the village and valley over countless centuries is somehow preserved in the walls, the trees, the very stones themselves, and the villagers have drunk in the legends, the superstitions and the realities of the ages. In Laurie Lee it shows itself in his attitude to outside authorities. The most tolerant and humane of writers, always ready to see in his own nature the follies and foibles he pokes fun at in others, he writes nevertheless with deep bitterness about what happened to Joseph and Hannah Brown. His compassion for them – for their mutual love, their dignity, their respect for all living things – boils into a fury of frustration, anger and bitterness: 'I was haunted by their end as by no other, and by the kind, killing Authority that arranged it'.

In 'Public Death, Private Murder' Lee admits to being enthralled by death, as a child; it was 'absorbing'. The section is filled with death, but it would be a mistake to feel it is all doom and gloom, for the villagers' (and his own) attitude to death was 'frank and unfear- ful'. So there is much humour in the section, too: the gossiping of the women after Miss Flynn's suicide (pp.101–2); how suicide could be contagious and during 'one particularly gloomy season even the coroner did himself in'; and the wonderful earthiness of Mr Davies – 'The Old Bugger seems to snatch 'em week-ends'; and (on his deathbed) 'When I'm gone, see I'm decent, missus. Wrap up me doings in a red silk handkerchief . . . .'

It is not just a question of humour, either, for it is clear that in the Lee household, as in almost any other, death (when it does not arouse deep emotions of grief or rage) is a very fit topic for gossip, for scandal, for a picking-over of the bizarre or gruesome details; so perhaps only in the last of the four anecdotes, the one in which Lee is wholly emotionally involved, is there no lighter element.

So to Miss Flynn, in whose story so many elements are combined. Hers was not the 'open and shut' case of the other three. Laurie has been kept in the dark about much that relates to Miss Flynn: 'Mother was evasive when we asked questions about her, and said, "There are others more wicked, pour soul"; '"and she half-gentry, too"'. Other women gossiped:

> '"She had a bit of a handicap, so they say."
> "You mean about those fellows?"
> "No, more'n that."'

Her attraction for Lee was clear – a 'pre-Raphaelite stunner', strange in her ways, clearly 'possessed', with an intriguing and unexplained past (and present?). Though Laurie did not see her drowned body, Fred Bates's description of how he found her works on his imagina- tion, producing one of the most beautiful poetic passages in the whole book:

> This was the pond that had choked Miss Flynn. Yet strangely, and
> not by accident. She had come to it naked, alone in the night, and
> had slipped into it like a bed; she lay down there, and drew the

water over her, and drowned quietly away in the reeds. I gazed at
the lily roots coiled deep down, at the spongy weeds around them.
That's where she lay, a green foot under, still and all night by
herself, looking up through the water as though through a window
and waiting for Fred to come by.

There is a final point worthy of consideration. The section is
headed 'Public Death, Private Murder'. Of the deaths in the four
stories, which was a public death, and which a private murder? Or
were any both? Or docs the heading have another meaning, too?

SECTION 7   MOTHER

Summary

Lee describes his mother in a totally single-minded way, and from as
many angles as he can remember. He tells her life story as far as he
knows it. There are three main phases. First is her 'working' life, her
single days. Having had to leave school early because her mother was
taken ill, she looked after her parents and many brothers until she
was seventeen. At this point she went into domestic service with 'the
gentry'. What she learned there of the way of life of the upper classes
remained with her all her days. After her mother's death, her father
became a public house landlord and Annie Light (as she still was)
came out of service to help him with the business. However the work
and responsibility devolved more and more upon her. Life was
passing her by. She decided to get out by answering an advertisement
in the local paper for a housekeeper to a young widower with four
children

This begins the second phase. She and the widower quickly fell in
love and married. Soon she had borne him four children, including
Laurie. The marriage was in every way a marriage of opposites,
however, and doomed to early failure. Her husband left her and,
alone, she brought up his first family along with the children they had
created together. The final phase of her life – another thirty-five
years or so – was taken up with the raising of the family and her
endless wait for the only man she had ever loved to come back to her,
even if (perhaps especially if) he was now weak and helpless. But Mr
Lee died, and with his death the hope that had sustained her life died
too. In only a short while she too was buried, near the cottage which
had been home for so long. Into this chronological account of her life,
however, Lee injects many anecdotes and memories of his mother

which build up a living picture of the woman whose life was so much a part of his. The personality of Mother Lee will be dealt with fully in the section on Technical Features.

Commentary

A quick count of the sections in *Cider with Rosie* reveals that there are thirteen; before this section there are six, and after it come a further six. In other words, the section 'Mother' is literally right in the middle of the book. Whether or not this is deliberate hardly matters, for the underlying reason is surely very clear: Mother Lee was the central fact in Laurie's life, the pivot round which everything revolved. Almost every section makes this clear; she belongs there – in the middle. The rest of this particular commentary will examine the debt Laurie owes his mother in shaping the kind of person he was to become. He himself, as one would expect of him, is quick to acknowledge all he gained from her, for his love of her shines on every page.

There is a very telling passage on pp.126–7 which will repay study:

> She fed our oafish wits with steady, imperceptible shocks of beauty . . . building up around us . . . an interpretation of man and the natural world so unpretentious and easy that we never recognized it then, yet so true that we never forgot it.
>
> Nothing now that I ever see that has the edge of gold around it . . . but my pleasure pays some brief duty to her . . . I absorbed from birth, as now I know, the whole earth through her jaunty spirit.

There are three noticeable qualities in this, each of them an enormous sector in the circle that makes up the total personality of Laurie Lee.

First, the 'interpretation of man'. This book is full of Lee's tolerance, his understanding, his humanity, his compassion; he accepts the human world readily, seeking always to understand rather than to condemn. He sees in man all the possibilities which he found fulfilled in his mother – dignity, delicacy of taste, sensibility, brightness of spirit, originality, indestructible gaiety, unshaken fidelities; (all of these terms Lee uses of his mother in this section).

Next is his love of the natural world, the world of bounty and harvest which at times seemed to take over their cottage: 'I often felt like an ant in a jungle, overwhelmed by its opulent clusters.' The book tumbles over with images of the joy Lee finds in the natural world around him. He writes that his mother, in her final days, 'snugly grew into her background, warm on her grassy bank, poking and peering among the flowery bushes, dishevelled and bright as they' – the beautiful merging of the woman with the world of nature.

That merging leads to the third quality – the finding of so much in life with 'the edge of gold' around it. Most of the examples he gives of this (p.127) are again taken from nature, but perhaps the finest illustration is to be found in the section quoted in the previous paragraph and taken from p.135. For here, Lee's mother is not far from madness, and indeed not far from death; yet in writing of this, how calm and golden a picture he creates: 'Serenely unkempt were those final years, free from conflict, doubt or dismay, while she reverted gently to a rustic simplicity as a moss-rose reverts to a wild one.' Truly Lee finds goodness and joy where many would miss it. He has a reverence for life that is akin to a religion, though not, of course, in any formal sense. Life is rich, life is full; everything it brings, every sight and sound, every experience, is to be savoured, sucked, milked until its essence is part of him.

Those three qualities, of course, go a long way towards creating an artist as well as a fully rounded human being, and it is easy to see how Lee would readily develop into a poet because of them. But this section identifies other traits too which Lee inherited from his mother, or grew up with, in her presence. She had a very amusing way with words, for instance, as is best seen in the impromptu rhyme and word-play she would break into on occasions; these had 'edge, economy, and freedom', Lee says. She greatly loved the written word, too – the Lee household was a literate one, with some books and multitudes of newspapers. One forever finds her lying on the floor cutting out items for her scrapbooks.

Music was a further joy to her. We hear of her solitary playing of the piano after the children were in bed, and singing; indeed she seems to break into song on any occasion, like the birds with whom he compares her. She passed on this love to Laurie who, as seen earlier, played the fiddle – well enough to make a rough living by playing on the streets in England, and then the length of Spain, as he recounts in his further autobiography, *As I Walked Out One Midsummer Morning*.

Things beautifully made appealed to her, especially old china, which she would buy even at the expense of food, such was her passion. A picture is built up, then, of a woman whose own artistic leanings were in some ways frustrated by force of circumstance, but whose creative instincts were passed on to Laurie.

Finally, a sad note. The love Laurie Lee had for his mother will be clear to every one of the millions who have read *Cider with Rosie*. But his tormenting thought is perhaps it remained unknown to her. As he lay in bed as a boy, listening to her playing the piano, he found the sounds almost 'shamefully moving. I wanted to run to her then, and embrace her as she played. But somehow I never did.'

SECTION 8   WINTER AND SUMMER

Summary

Lee points out how the city or town-dweller, especially in recent times, has become less and less aware of the differences between the seasons; all somehow merge into one, since there is little, apart from outside temperature, to signal a change. How different things were in Slad village in the early 1920s, when the seasons 'broke into our houses' and 'ordered our lives'. This section develops these differences, distilling summers and winters into an essence of each. Memories and recollections are recounted from winter and summer in turn.

Winter was the time for boys to devise new and exciting outdoor activities: falling about on the ice of Jones's pond; helping Farmer Wells in his cowshed; chasing through the frozen lands on imaginary steeds; listening to his sisters tell of 'disasters' in the snow and ice that they have encountered at work in Stroud; then, as Christmas approached, making their annual carol-singing tour of the local farms and estates, for Laurie belonged to the Church Choir (a rather grand title for a handful of boys whose singing was less than inspiring!) But at their final port of call, Farmer Joseph's, somehow Christmas became real to them all, its meaning as sparklingly clear as the star-riddled sky above them.

Then comes summer – suddenly it is there, and it is as if things have never been otherwise. Now the days are spent languidly in the lazy heat; eating sherbet, drinking from the cool spring, lying in the long grass, gazing at the blue sky and hearing the myriads of insects, busy as ever; and playing an occasional frenetic game of cricket at Sixpence Robinson's farm cottage. When the energy-sapping heat of the day is over, there are night games to play. Animal calls would bring the other village boys creeping out of their beds; a hunting game, Fox and Hounds, would be organised, with two boys being tracked by all the rest; there were no boundaries: they were as free to roam the countryside as the wild creatures whose cries they imitated.

Commentary

This section is a collection of memories, grouped round a topic or theme; in this respect it is little different from several of the other sections. On this occasion, the recollections are evoked by one observation: that in the rural life of his childhood the difference in the seasons was so highly marked as to require a completely different way of life among the villagers. However, Lee does not view winter and summer in the same way as most British people – that summer is wonderful with its warmth, whereas the short, freezing days of winter are unpleasant. Even a casual reading of this book, or this section, should dispel any such thoughts.

As was pointed out in the section 'Mother', Lee finds goodness and joy where many would miss it. The joy he finds in the games and activities of winter is every bit as great as that which he finds in summer. Of course the experiences are different, but not less enjoyable. Only visually is winter less rich than summer, for the land is taken over by a uniform grey-whiteness; but with all his other senses Lee responds as powerfully to the one as to the other. It is perhaps worth noting here that the more things in life one takes joy from, the more enjoyable will be one's life. Lee would see it as almost our duty to enjoy *all* the sensations and experiences of life; to him, the smell of 'green dung' in the cow byre is as rich (in all senses!) as the smell of the sweetest wild rose. Life is wonderful – savour it; that seems to be the constant message of *Cider with Rosie*.

There are two further points, related to this last and to each other, which should be made about this section. First is the animal-like activity of the young Laurie. (This occurs elsewhere in the book, and Lee also compares his mother with the birds: 'mischievous as a chimney-jackdaw'; 'made her nest of rags and jewels'; 'squawked loudly at danger'; 'lived by the laws of the hedgerow'; indeed her supreme quality as a woman is that she has never lost in adulthood the natural qualities of a bird – or a child.) We see him as he 'galloped away down the road, bucking and snorting'; the 'boys went calling along the roads, wild slit-eyed animal calls'; 'padding softly, we ran'; 'following the scent'. This sense of being part of the whole animal world is surely one of the factors which brings a sense of harmony to life itself.

Second is the enormous pleasure Lee takes in the simplest of activities. All the 'entertainment' which he and his friends or family found came first from within themselves; in this section, if one asks the crudely simple question, 'What did they actually do?' the answer, in one sense, is 'Precious little'. But then again one might answer,

'They didn't need to *do* – they simply *were*'. This is perhaps not an easy concept to understand, but it means that just to be alive is the joy. As Lee says of summer: 'There was nothing to do. Nothing moved or happened, nothing happened at all except summer.' Summer *was*, and he *was* – part of it, within it, living it; in that was the pleasure. In the very first section of the book, on p.17, he puts the case beautifully: 'I was awake, I could see, I was happy.'

SECTION 9 SICK BOY

Summary

As an infant young Laurie Lee had the curious distinction of being baptised twice, the first time within a day or two of his birth, for he seemed very likely to live for only a very short time. The second time, a little more conventionally, was when he was three. The rest of this section takes up the topic of his childhood illnesses, which were many and serious. The deaths of children were all too frequent experiences for parents: Laurie's father had already buried three babies and Laurie's own sister Frances died when she was four. He remembers at least one death-bed vigil at his own bedside. The fact that he did survive, however, convinced him that, though he was not strong, he was tough.

Much of the section describes the strange world of bed-ridden illness, with its fantasies and nightmares, its daydreams and imaginings. He recounts again a situation that has cropped up before, in which he imagines himself King; this time his subjects are gravely concerned for his health. Illness, however, makes those times when he is well a kind of bonus, to be fully enjoyed; he is grateful for life. The section ends on a curious note. All his illnesses, he writes, had a less lasting effect on him than an accident he had when, after being knocked down by a bicycle one dark night, he lay unconscious for two days. Ever since, he has been subject to strange mental visitations.

Commentary

This is another of the sections in *Cider with Rosie* in which Lee, having started on a particular topic, reminisces about it in a fairly random way. His topic this time – his frequent illnesses as a child – is a little unusual in that, although all of the book is in some sense about Laurie Lee, very seldom does he concentrate on himself and his own preoccupations as he does in this section. Perhaps illness inevitably makes us turn in on ourselves. But it should be made clear that there is not a trace in this section of self-pity or sympathy-seeking: it is as full of the joy of living as any of the other sections.

In commenting on some other sections of *Cider with Rosie* frequent use has been made of a fairly simple psychological approach, in an attempt to discover how the writer Laurie Lee, who is seen in action as the writer of the book, is a natural and logical product of the experiences of his early days, of his background, of his family circumstances, and so on. What he 'inherited' from his mother is obviously a good example of this. In this section there are three further such 'clues'.

The first concerns his sister Frances, who died when she was four, and he was a mere eighteen months old. Frances was the daughter for whom Laurie's mother cried almost daily all her life – the only girl she produced in a life which was dominated by brothers and sons. The passage in this section in which Frances dies is a very poignant one; she seemed to have developed a special love for her sick baby brother, sitting watchfully over him like a nurse, talking to him in a special language of her own. That Frances was herself dying seems to have gone unnoticed, so concerned was the family with Laurie. She died 'suddenly, silently, without complaint, in a chair in the corner of the room'. Then Lee writes (and this is the point): 'I believe she gave me her life.' What a debt to carry! What an obligation, to feel a life has been given for you! So he survives, determinedly, and makes sure that the life he has been given is not wasted, but crammed full of all that life has to offer, as if he were living Frances's life for her, too. The richness of his life, seen in the richness of his writings, is in part at least due to the feeling that there is a debt to be paid.

The second point is a somewhat similar one. For years, as this section recalls, Laurie was racked by fevers, lung problems, and many other serious illnesses. (This is probably the last thing you would have imagined, before reaching this point of the book.) Months could be spent combating the illness and then recuperating from it. Yet recuperate he always did, of course; what is of concern now is his own response to his recoveries. He makes his feeling clear on p.166: 'Each morning at dawn I lay in a trance of thanks'. When you have almost lost something it becomes especially dear: even a boiled egg 'tasted of sun-warmed manna'. Here too may be mentioned the strange concluding paragraph of the section, in which he feels that the two-day concussion he experienced after being knocked down set free all manner of hidden forms within him, inducing at times a near insanity, a heightened sensitivity to the darker world of the mind's deepest recesses. The result of all this, of course, is seen again in his writings: because, so often, he had been at death's door, his love of life was the stronger. This zest for living, this enthusiasm for the whole splendid tapestry of life, is the most noticeable feature of *Cider with Rosie*.

The third point is perhaps even more directly connected with the nature of much of his writing. The reader can hardly have failed to notice that almost all of Lee's description, whether of animate or inanimate objects, is closely observed to a quite extraordinary degree. This habit of intense observation appears to stem directly from the amount of time he lay on his back in bed – not so much when he was ill, perhaps, as when he was getting better. This section alone provides much evidence to support this idea. On p.162, for instance, his ear is attuned to every sound: 'birds folding their wings, a hill-sheep's cough, a far gate swinging, the breath of a horse in a field', and so on, through many more details. Again, on p.166, as he lies awake in the morning, he 'sensed, without needing to look, the state of the early day . . . that there were cows in the field or not, whether the garden gate was open or shut . . . the weight of the clouds in the invisible sky'. He is taken over entirely by his senses; since he is physically confined to bed, he can only live through his senses: through what he can see, touch, taste, smell and hear. This must have helped develop the sensuous awareness that is to be found throughout the book.

As a final point – to be developed more fully later – it is worth mentioning the great humour in this section. It is perhaps very typical of the writer as we see him in this book that he is more prepared to make fun of himself than of anyone else, and to find comedy in times of greatest personal adversity.

SECTION 10   THE UNCLES

Summary

Laurie Lee describes in turn his mother's five brothers. What they seem to have had in common, with the possible exception of Fred, the last, was a larger-than-life character, a habit of hard drinking, an attraction for women, and a zest for living. They had inherited from their father, a coachman, an expertise with horses, and would possibly have made their own living in that world had not outside influences interfered, in the shape of two wars; two of the brothers fought in both, all five in the second. To Laurie they were all heroes. In his earliest memories they merge into one figure, a ghost in military uniform who for a few days would share their home and then be off to war again. Later, however, he separates them, and writes of each in turn.

Charlie had fought in the Boer War as well as in the First World War. He had lived an adventurous, exotic and in some ways mysterious life in South Africa after the Boer War. On returning home he became a forester. Lee feels that the woods he planted, now well established and flourishing, are his memorial, for he died the year before Lee wrote *Cider with Rosie*.

Ray was perhaps the most extraordinary. He had taken himself off to Canada and been employed in a variety of tough jobs, including the laying of the Canadian Pacific Railway. A huge, tattooed, leathery, sun-tanned figure, he was a genuine adventurer, who flirted outrageously with Laurie's half-sisters – and other girls – in between bouts of heavy drinking, in the best pioneer spirit.

Sid, too, was a great drinker. A small, powerful man, he was a bus-driver at a time when the double-decker was the acknowledged king of the road. His drinking, however, led to many cautions from his employers, and eventually to his dismissal. Whenever he was in trouble, he would make a fake, laughably insincere, suicide attempt.

Like Charlie, Tom served in both the Boer War and the First World War. He was something of a dandy, relentlessly pursued by girls as a young man – and eventually caught, to become a coach-man-gardener. The last brother, Fred, was clearly unknown to Laurie, 'lost through prosperity and distance', and he leaves him undescribed.

Commentary

Four splendid characters (we can hardly count Fred) illuminate this section – in some ways one of the lightest sections of the book. The character of Laurie's mother is hardly surprising when seen alongside these men, for they share many of her traits. Nor is it surprising, of course, that since they are like her in many respects Laurie should give them his hero-worship when a boy, and profound admiration when a man. His affection for his uncles is a real guide to the character of the writer himself; they are a living picture of what he finds best in mankind.

All had a great zest and enthusiasm for life's pleasures, a physical exuberance. They worked with their muscles, doing hard manual work (even bus-driving required strength in those days!). They were men's men, prepared to cross the world to fight in South Africa, and to endure, even with wry humour, the hardships and suffering of the First World War. That Sid should knock down an unknown man because he was physically bullying a woman seems to me typical of the whole family, combining a sense of justice and a sense of chivalry with a love of action.

Mostly they were outdoor men, too, working with the soil, the rock, or animals; men who built – whether railways, woods or gardens. Sid is not to be seen as an exception to this. When he 'wrenched and wrestled at the steering wheel to hold the great bus on its course' his actions are just as 'heroic' as Ray's, dynamiting his way through the Canadian mountains to build the great railroad.

Though Lee implies that Fred is being omitted from the general description because he lives further off (the rest have resettled in the area) and has become prosperous, there is perhaps a third reason – he was an insurance man! In the company of such men as the other four, how could an 'office' man ever seem other than an anti-climax? What Lee writes about Fred's prosperity is also worthy of mention. There is a clear suggestion, that like so many people who 'get on' in the world, Fred dropped his family, who were in more humble situations, and that Laurie Lee disapproves of this. There are times in the book when one feels that Lee has a deep mistrust of the gentry and the wealthy, and constantly takes sides with the exploited, the common working man. In this section, for instance, we read of Uncle Charlie: 'His employers flattered, cherished, and *underpaid* him'. This skilful craftsman of the woods 'raised his family *on labourer's pay*'. These are comments about social justice.

There is one other issue to broach here, though it will be examined in more detail elswhere, and that is the nostalgia which is so prominent in the book. It is natural, of course, that if a middle-aged man chooses to write a book about his own early years, he is likely to be nostalgic for his personal past. But in *Cider with Rosie* Lee's nostalgia extends far beyond this, to become a nostalgia for a whole age that has gone. When the book's final sections are considered the subject will crop up again, because it features strongly there, but in this section there are powerful foretastes.

In particular we glimpse the way in which the Boer War, and then more especially the First World War, marked the end of an era. Though none of the Light brothers was killed – a remarkable case in itself – their lives and ways of life were radically altered. One remained for a time where war had cast him up – in South Africa. Another made his way to Canada. The physical boundaries of their vision had been widened. It is true, of course, that they returned; but the old way of life had gone, too. These men were brought up to work with horses, as their father, the Berkeley coachman, had done; in any previous generation for the past nine hundred years or so, that is

what they would have done. But war, and the internal combustion
engine, changed all that: 'They were the horsemen and brawlers of
another age, and their lives spoke its long farewell . . . a world that
still moved at the same pace as Caesar's, and . . . that Em-
pire . . . [of] which they had . . . seen the first outposts crumble'.

Life would never be the same again.

SECTION 11 OUTINGS AND FESTIVALS

Summary

The section begins with a short description of the way in which the
cycle of nature in the seasons is reflected in a whole series of
'revolutions' connected with the village and involving the village
itself, the festivals, the church and the Squire. Then follow the
descriptions of three specific village 'occasions' which Lee has
remembered and, sandwiched among them, a telescoped memory of
family outings. Whole days would be spent gathering wild fruit from
the countryside around, to be converted into pies, jams, preserves; or
on outings to visit Uncle Charlie and his family in their cottage in the
woods at Sheepscombe; it was always a great delight to play freely in
the less familiar surroundings.

The first of the specific village occasions he recalls is Peace Day,
1919, an official celebration of the ending of the First World War.
The whole village sported itself in fancy dress, with Laurie as John
Bull, and the proverbial 'good time was had by all', except perhaps
Poppy Green who, though dressed as an angel with wings, proved
unable to fly when Laurie knocked her off the mantelpiece. (Not the
only occasion on which he inflicted violence on a little girl.)

The second particular village occasion was an annual Church Choir
Outing, this time to Weston-super-Mare. On previous trips of this
kind, horses had pulled them on farm wagons to Gloucester, but this
was a charabanc outing (five charabancs, in fact, for the whole village
went). The events of the day are related in detail, with the reader's
impressions being of the great sense of adventure; the excitement of
newness; the exhilaration of speed felt by those sitting on top of the
coach; and the community spirit of the villagers, facing together an
alien, more sophisticated world.

Finally, there was the Parochial Church Tea and Annual Entertainment, a hilarious mixture of gluttonous feasting and home-spun
'turns' from the villagers, plus a guest 'artiste'. Laurie himself took
part, playing the fiddle, as did his sisters in various sketches. These,

then, were some of the special times in the life of Slad Village, which
Laurie Lee never forgot.

Commentary

Earlier sections 'Public Death, Private Murder' and 'The Uncles'
illustrated the tightly-knit life of a community such as Slad. If,
however, one feels that a principal theme of *Cider with Rosie* is the
passing of an age (as it surely is) then it is in this section that one is
most conscious of that passing, at least in so far as it concerned the
village. First of all we see two major influences on village life which
have, for the most part, disappeared. One of these was the squire,
who for centuries had been the dominating figure in rural life, for
good or ill; he was the greatest landowner, he lived in the largest
house, he was the principal employer, he was the richest villager, and
possibly the best-educated too. Lee's Squire is an old man, sentimental, not completely in his right mind, doddery – ideally suited,
perhaps, to be the last of his line. Even in such major village
occasions as this section describes, Lee seems to see him already as an
irrelevance.

The second influence was the established church, the Church of
England. It is probably very hard for us now to envisage the great
power the Church had in England. It pervaded all aspects of life. Of
course in *Cider with Rosie* one hears little of the church and so is led
to believe that Lee was not in a narrow sense religious. But he did, as
a boy, go to church every Sunday – more than once, as he was in the
choir – and the beginning of this section shows very clearly how the
revolving cycle of the church's year, seen in the great festivals of
Easter, Whitsuntide, the Harvest and Christmas, corresponded to,
and was interlinked with, the changing seasons of the natural year.
But Lee's vicar cuts a somewhat foolish figure, out of touch with
everyday realities and unable to relate to the people; (his leaden,
sombre 'jokes' at the Entertainment; his failure to join the whole
village on a Church Outing, and his hope that they would spend a few
moments in a church at Weston-super-Mare all show him to be
remote from the lives of the villagers.) Like the Squire, with whom he
traditionally had very strong links, the vicar seems to be losing his
relevance.

Next we see that the village still had a vital sense of its own unity
(the Church and Squire of course were strong unifying elements).
Everyone knew everyone else; when they left the confines of their
valley *en masse* on an outing it was 'Slad versus the Rest of the
World'. This is still true of some of the remoter corners of England,

but greater and easier communications; the mobility brought about by the normality of car-ownership; the wider vision of the world promoted by such things as television and package holidays; the greater financial independence; and, sadly, sometimes the economic necessity of moving to find work; all of these have combined to change the face and nature of village life in ways in which it had not been changed for centuries. That process is already at work in *Cider with Rosie*; it is seen at its simplest in the shift from horse-drawn carts for their outings to motorised charabancs. The short ride to Gloucester can now become the hitherto unthinkable day-trip to Weston.

Finally there is a sense of adventure and excitement. The people of Slad rarely moved outside the village; there was neither need nor opportunity. More importantly, perhaps, the world outside intruded very little on their lives. It is difficult to imagine how confining it was to live in such a world; you may never have seen a large town; you would not have been familiar with the wonders of the whole world through the media of film or television; you would never have been to a theatre to see a play or music-hall; you may never even have seen the sea. It is in this light that we must see how magical were what might seem to us rather mundane events; these 'outings and festivals' were anticipated with excitement for weeks, prepared for, savoured to the full when they arrived, and picked over in conversation until the next one. Such simple joy and fun have probably largely disappeared.

SECTION 12   FIRST BITE AT THE APPLE

Summary

In this section Lee mainly recalls his first sexual encounters with girls, from the time he was eleven or twelve, though the section makes another interesting point too. First of the girls he experimented with was Jo. She was younger than him, and a willing but totally passive and silent partner in the games of 'doctor and patient' which they played after school on grassy banks in the valley. Sooner or later, of course, they were bound to be discovered – in this case by a couple of farm-hands, who treated the situation as high comedy.

It is at this point that Lee turns aside for a couple of pages from the principal material of his section to make a sweeping comment on 'crime and punishment'. The gist of his view is that the young people of his village were able to grow up in a natural way, without the intervention and interference of outside authority. If punishment was required for a particular transgression, then the villagers or parents provided it; it could be over and done with in a few minutes, or in some cases could last for years.

He then turns to Rosie Burdock, describing the encounter which gave the book its title. Following this is the strange case of what he calls the Brith Wood rape, though no physical contact took place at all, when Laurie and a gang of cronies decided to rape a local, eccentric girl (though they seem to have had little or no knowledge of what they would actually do!). When Lizzie Berkeley appeared, however, the plan fizzled out after a half-hearted attempt to stand in her way. (She simply clouted Bill, the leader, with a bag of crayons.) The section ends with an epilogue: an updating of what had eventually become of each of the main participants in the section.

Commentary

To write about adolescent sexuality, except in a purely scientific or psychological way, is never easy. It is especially difficult to write about one's own early experiments and experiences, as Lee does here. Yet from a 'literary' point of view, this section is a triumph. Though at times the sensuality of the situations is very powerful, there is never a hint of crudeness or cheapness; nor is there, on the other hand, any attempt to gloss over, with a soft-focus, romantic-sentimental approach, such simple realities as the twelve-year-old Laurie Lee's hands exploring the contours of a younger girl's naked body. Such words as 'delicacy' are not appropriate here to describe the writing; they suggest a shying away from something as if it were a matter for shame, or an unwillingness to look reality in the face. Rather, Lee's success in handling his topic rests on three qualities in the writing.

The first of these is humour. Lee has a very self-mocking kind of humour; he looks back at his naivety, his inexperience, his fumbling awkwardness, and spreads it out for us to enjoy too – as in the episode with Jo. He captures exactly the bragging bravado of boys when they are in a gang, and is prepared to smile shamefacedly at their 'scruffy' plan for Lizzy. The 'epilogue' is full of neatly ironic humour when what happened later to these young people is recounted. And of course the whole erotic escapade with Rosie is told with such zestful sexual excitement that the joy of it all becomes its own humour.

The second of these qualities is his natural honesty about sex. This has been evident elsewhere in the book, too. The growth of sexual awareness is a natural part of healthy growing up. A few brief quotations from the section will illustrate this: 'Such early sex-games were formal exercises, the hornless charging of calves'; 'the landscape abounded with natural instruction'; 'They received me naturally, the boys and girls of my age, and together we entered the tricky wood'; 'curiosity [was] our first concern'; 'awkward, convulsed, but *never surreptitious*'; 'all of that green age . . . unformed . . . and coldly innocent'. What is happening is hardly more than play-acting: 'we imitated as best we could'; 'we did little more than mime the realities'; 'The girls played their part of invitation and show'. He and Jo are doctor and patient. It is all a mere short step from the child's world of Cowboys and Indians (or their current equivalent) and dolls in prams – and just as natural, just as normal.

This leads to the third of the qualities, which I can only describe as sound common sense. Lee is strongly resentful of the kind of outside authority which seeks to interfere with, and govern, our lives. In one of the most powerful and deeply felt sections in the whole book, on pp.205–6, he again launches an attack, all the more startling because it springs out of nothing, as if a seething oil-well of emotion has suddenly been uncapped. His anger is clear, and it is aimed at the law and its agents:–the magistrates, the 'coppers'. They would have defined Laurie and Jo as 'obscene' for their youthful experiments. Most of the boys of the villages, he writes, 'at some stage . . . of our growth, would have been rounded up . . . and quite a few shoved into reform school' – a statistic in the book of a 'cold-mouthed copper'. And then, in a searing shaft: 'The modern city, for youth, is a police-trap.' Powerful stuff!

What, then, is his 'sound common sense' answer? It is to leave the communities to be their own magistrates – not in an official sense, of course, but in all those ways in which a community can voice its feelings; it is to view 'crime' with understanding. He does not pretend that Slad had no statutory crime with regard to sexual, and other, offences; but note the understsanding he shows in such statements as: 'Quiet incest flourished where the roads were bad'; 'Drink, anim-ality, and rustic boredom were responsible for most'; 'I was one of a green-horned gang . . . confused by our strength and boredom'. The point, however, is that the village dealt with its own; it 'neither approved nor disapproved, but neither did it complain to authority. Sometimes our sinners were given hell, taunted, and pilloried' but it was all kept within the village.

The villagers' attitude to the sexual romping of the young boys and girls in this section, put at its simplest in the face of an interfering authority would be: 'For goodness' sake, they are just kids. Kids always have been curious about sex; they always will be, thank God!

No harm is done, and probably a lot has been learned. Just leave them alone – *we* can handle them.'

Finally, to link this to the rather odd incident of the Brith Wood rape, what comes out of that episode is that something within the boys tells them that what they are planning to do is just not right. The magistrate is inside themselves; they do not abandon the affair out of fear, but because it suddenly seems sordid and squalid: 'the bounce had somehow gone out of us'. When they thought Lizzy was not coming they 'began to cheer up and giggle'. When she arrived, 'Bill and Boney went sickly pale and watched her in utter misery.'

SECTION 13   LAST DAYS

Summary

This last section begins with a reflection on the fact that Lee's childhood happened to be at the time when the life of the village, which had scarcely changed over the centuries, finally disintegrated. The fastest feasible pace had been the speed of a horse – eight miles per hour. But with the coming of the motor car, motor bike and bus, the old ways were doomed; the valley would be opened up, gradually to take its place in the mainstream of existence.

As is often the case when a human being dies, however, there was a last-gasp show of strength in the village. Lee describes how the twin pillars of village life, the Church and the Squire, still exerted their powerful influence: every Sunday saw the villagers going to church as naturally as, next day, they would do the family washing; the role of the Squire seemed to be as strong as ever – even if the present Squire was not. But when he died the big house was auctioned off and became an institution; similarly the new ideas from the wide world outside ended the unquestioning faith and obedience which had always been given to the church. The appointment of a new, 'modern' vicar buried the Church's authority completely. Old people gradually died off too – 'the last of their world'.

Next Lee describes the inevitable break-up of his own family, when the courting days of his sisters and his elder brother, Harold, began. The first such event, coinciding as it did with a fire at the boiler-works, is recalled in detail, as is the disastrous picnic the family, plus boy-friends, went on one fiercely hot Sunday. The last three paragraphs of the book come back to Laurie Lee himself. The strange feverish melancholy of adolescence is upon him, the 'madness' of youth, when his own destiny was being worked out; the urge to

compose his thoughts, his words, into poetry was overpowering. The
string of dots which end the book are an indication that his story was
not yet finished; (he was at that point still a teenager, though that
word had not yet been coined). He continues his autobiography in
the wonderful book already alluded to, *As I Walked Out One
Midsummer Morning*, dealing with his incredible solitary journey
from Slad to London, to the coast, and then right through Spain,
when he was only nineteen. It is an exciting, revealing book.

Commentary

The title of this final section. 'Last Days', has at least three separate
areas of references: these years were, of course, the last days in the
real childhood, the innocent time, of Laurie Lee himself; they were
also the last days of the family unit that had been the Lee household,
for by the end of the book all three of his sisters are on the verge of
leaving home, Harold is a working man, and Laurie himself seeks the
solitary places where he can come to terms with his growing
consciousness of himself as a separate, unique individual, and give
free rein to his burning creative urge; finally they were the last days of
the village as he had known it.

This last point can be handled first. In the section 'The Kitchen' the
kitchen became a symbolic character in Lee's mind when he thought
back on his family life. Now, perhaps, the village too has become a
symbolic character; but whereas the kitchen was part of the family,
an appropriate symbol for the warm cosiness, the suffocating fug so
much at the centre of Laurie's early life, the village is a symbol of
something altogether bigger, wider, and – in the final analysis – more important; it is a symbol more appropriate to the greater
maturity and broader vision of Lee's later years.

Throughout the book, the sense of nostalgia is strong. The village
is here the focal point for that nostalgia; more clearly even than in
'Outings and Festivals' Lee shows us how the passing of his childhood
coincided with the passing of a whole, and very ancient, way of life. It
is well worth re-reading the second paragraph of this section – slowly – to try to take in the enormity of what was happening.

What is Lee's attitude to the death of 'his' village? We can only
begin by saying that his feelings are mixed. On the one hand, he does
write of it as a 'death', and deaths are not normally causes of
celebration. Moreover, in his mind that death is knottily entangled
with the 'death' of his own childhood, and the 'death' of his family as
an unbroken unit. In describing how the old folk simply 'dropped
away' he uses such sad imagery as: 'Kicker Harris . . . blew away like

a torn-out page'. Some of his memories of the church as it was are tinged with deep affection, too, especially his reminiscences about Evensong, when the church was sincere and intimate, when the social protocol of the morning service was gone, when quiet peace reigned; and in his memories of the Harvest Festivals, when the bringing of the fruits of nature into the church seemed to him a gesture far older than Christianity itself – man's gratitude to his gods, not his God, and his public statement of fellowship with the whole village community.

On the other hand, however, the villagers had grown up for centuries in ignorance of the great world beyond the valley. 'That eight miles an hour was life and death, the size of our world, our prison'. Gloucester, 'once a foreign city', was now a quick trip. Along with the shrinking distances, of course, came new ideas: 'free thought, and new excitements, came now to intrigue and perplex us': a couple dared to marry in a registry office, instead of in the church; and he himself was severely censured for reading *Sons and Lovers* (the D. H. Lawrence novel which has for long been a standard school text). Perhaps the most telling factor on this side of the balance is that Lee has presented all through *Cider with Rosie* his sense of the vigour and unstoppable urges of growth seen in all areas of the natural world; growth, by definition, means change; always the old order must give way to new.

It is true that Lee cannot help but look back with warmth at things long past – many of them personal and dear; but he would not have wanted it any other way. The book does end, after all, with a series of humorous pictures of the courtship of his sisters, which suggests that he does not wish to become too bogged down in regret. There seems now to have been a rush of days: no sooner has the first boyfriend arrived on the scene (for Marjorie) than Dorothy and Phyllis produce theirs; courtships quickly blossom into engagements and in a very short space plans for marriage are being made – maybe the changed pace is symptomatic of life's faster march.

The final paragraphs deserve comment here, too. One feels the call of the outside world beckoning to Laurie. It is almost time for him to be on the move, to take his place in the adult world. His life, up to now so preoccupied with his family and friends, now turns in on itself; he is beset by all manner of passions; his emotional life is topsy-turvy; he sails on a frenzied sea. Yet somewhere there is a powerful creative stirring within him, to give to his passions the life of words. A young poet is in the melting-pot.

3 THEMES AND ISSUES

3.1 EARTH AND NATURE

The theme of the vitality and richness of a life lived close to the earth and nature is very powerful. The message which life seems to have passed on to Laurie Lee is that human experience is as limitless as the earth's produce, there to be enjoyed, constantly renewed with a perennial freshness. *Cider with Rosie* abounds in piled-up images of natural things. But there are many smaller, particular matters, which show how all-pervasive is the natural world. The very first picture of Laurie Lee sees him totally immersed in long grass – perhaps a symbolic image in itself! In no time his sisters are stuffing him full of berries – the natural bounty of the earth – as birds cram the ever-open mouths of their young. The garden becomes his first teacher, showing him its endless variety; here too he learns to cope with the decaying process, the natural law which says not only that all living things must die but that through death new life is created: rotting leaves feed the soil with goodness, a dead cat provides food for hosts of grubs. He discovers, too, the magical properties of the elements, especially water, with which one can do so many things: 'confine or scatter, or send down holes'; 'drink it, draw with it . . . fly it in bubbles'; but 'never burn or break or destroy'. Such curiosity, such inquiring, takes him to the elemental heart of life itself.

Much concerning the natural world is learned from those people he comes into contact with, of course. Foremost among these is his mother, but we should not forget Granny Wallon, whose part of the house was constantly piled high with all manner of crops for her wine-making; nor Granny Trill, whose life was lived as if she were a creature of the woods, rising with the dawn chorus and returning early to her nest. Her father's great beech tree gave Laurie a first inkling of the vast improbabilities of time. The background of the Light family was totally rural; their work was in rural craft and industry; though Laurie's uncles, by force of circumstance, were mostly hived off into other forms of employment, they were nevertheless always comfortable in the countryside, familiar and at ease there, as if that were their habitat.

Although the care of horses had been the family 'business', animals hardly feature in *Cider with Rosie*, either as farm animals or domestic pets. The emphasis is always on the productive side of Nature: the staples of bread, berries, vegetables, home-made wines, and of course cider; perhaps in no other drink is the connection so direct between the ingredients and the final product: the full, heady taste of the pressed apples, the mind-spinning incense-like smell, the down-to-earth realness of cider, are the perfect combination, along with Rosie, to introduce Laurie to the pleasures of that other basic matter – the delights of physical contact with the opposite sex.

This 'direct connection' between Man and Nature requires comment. One of the ways in which our Western world has changed so much since Lee's childhood is in the severing of that direct connection, and Lee is clearly very conscious of this. Though we can still go to a greengrocer's and buy fresh fruit and vegetables (indeed, in much greater variety than was possible before) we are at least as likely to buy them in packets, or tins, or even frozen; and our 'fresh' produce must be thoroughly washed to cleanse it of chemical sprays. For Mrs Lee, vegetables came from her garden or her neighbour, or the farmer; and it was with this situation that Laurie grew up. Precisely because one plucked one's own apples, or dug up one's own carrots, the link between Earth the provider and Man the consumer was simple and powerful; the canning factory, the freezer company, the packaging firm, played no part in it. Laurie Lee understood the natural world of growth, and responded so strongly to it because of that bond. 'Mother' Nature would not be an embarrassingly rustic phrase for him but a simple reality. Somewhere in all this is a religious element (using 'religious' in a wide sense) to be examined more closely later in this section.

3.2 GROWING UP

A second major theme of the book is inevitably that of the early development of the author, and the factors which combine to make a unique individual human being. Such a theme has constant relevance:

there will always be children. More important, all great literature is an exploration of the human condition, a probing of the human heart and mind; childhood has perhaps been rather neglected in literature, or at least the searching inquiry into the growing-up process has not often been handled in depth. Let us then look at three aspects of Laurie Lee's growth.

3.2.i The mother–son relationship

The mother–son relationship, psychologists tell us, is the strongest of all bonds, and certainly Laurie was very tightly bound to his mother. Family circumstances no doubt tied the knot even more tightly than usual, since he had neither a father nor a father-figure, in practical terms; indeed he came under other powerful female influences besides his mother's. What difference, if any, did this make? It must be re-stated that Laurie was in no way 'feminised' by his circumstances. Perhaps having a brother as his 'close companion' was his saving grace in this. Nevertheless, he inherited from his mother (from his constant contact with her, as well as genetically) many of the qualities and leanings which developed his artistic temperament, as well as a view of life which he retained in adult life. His desire to please her, to win her approval (by his violin-playing, for instance) was strong. His life would certainly have developed very differently had his father featured normally in it – especially as his father was in many ways the antithesis of his mother.

His relationship with her is not static, however; it grows, develops, shifts. Initially he is inseparable from her; she is 'the presence for whom one had moaned and hungered'; the 'wordless nights' in her bed are 'like a secret I held through the waking day'. But from her, when Tony took his place, he learned his 'first lesson in the gentle, merciless rejection of women'. The very slow process which takes place through the book is of course the change from a subjective view of his mother to an objective one; the beautiful element of the relationship is that, as he grows up, as he looks back on his mother from his mid-40s, the bond he feels, the love he gives, are even stronger than in his blind childhood days. He has willingly replaced the apron-strings of their blood-relationship with the love-chain of fellow-feeling.

3.2.ii The social experience of growing up

This is the gradual growth of an understanding that the world was not made for you alone. For Laurie Lee this was a straightforward enough process. As one of a large family, he had to share resources, food, affection; his was not the only call on his mother's time; Tony took his bed-place, Jack took his share of supper. Not for Laurie the luxury of a room of his own – if luxury it is; yet though the house was full it was 'never I think . . . overcrowded.'

From his immediate family, then, came his first awareness of the need to integrate. His boundaries were widened when he went to school; his schooldays provided his 'first amazed vision of any world outside . . . my family'. Socially, what did he learn there? Much, certainly, of what is permissible and what is not in social behaviour; much, also, when he went into the 'Big Room' about the harsher realities of life – the bullying, the greed, the selfishness. But he learned other, more positive, things: the warmth of companionship with the other boys of his gang, their 'indivisible maleness'; the different, strange ways and life-styles of the 'wild boys and girls from miles around – from the outlying farms and half-hidden hovels'; a sense of justice; a feeling of compassion for the poor and suffering; the curious, pleasurable warmth of the company of girls other than his sisters.

School was not his whole existence, of course; in fact it plays a minor part in the book as a whole. Other experiences reinforced his growing social awareness too: the church choir and annual carol-singing; the outings into the world beyond the village; summer and winter activities with his friends, in the fields and on the ice, in daylight and after dark. He also meets, and has to come to terms with, the facts of death, suicide, and even murder; with men drunk, with men fighting; he encounters the very old at close quarters, and the eccentric too. Perhaps because of his small village upbringing he knew, in real terms, more people than would a child reared in the anonymous city. Certainly he becomes a writer thoroughly acquainted with all that is best – and some of what is worst – in humanity.

3.2.iii The growth of sexual awareness

Laurie Lee learned very quickly that the quality of femaleness is very different from maleness. His early experience is of course entirely with the family, but even here he responds from infancy to the soft, slow, rounded warmth of his mother and sisters. This is, of course, perfectly normal, but possibly more keenly developed in Laurie because he had four females, not just one, to turn to, and all of them were 'givers', with powerful maternal instincts. These family circumstances surely provide one major reason why Laurie is so keenly interested in the opposite sex as the book progresses.

He is very drawn to his first young Infant teacher – her physical presence is intensely pleasurable – probably because she is of an age with Marjorie and Dorothy. She could almost be described as yet another mother to him. Even at this stage, however, he was attracted to girls of his own age, the first he has met: 'two blonde girls, already puppyishly pretty, whose names and bodies were to distract and haunt me for the next fifteen years of my life. Poppy and Jo . . . '. From early years, boys have a natural, usually healthy curiosity about girls (and vice-versa) – especially their bodies. We see this in several episodes in *Cider with Rosie*. When Laurie's next teacher says, 'If you only could watch me getting dressed in the morning you'd know it wasn't' (a wig) she 'stirred my imagination' – the suggestion seemed 'both outrageous and wonderful.' Laurie and his gang shout from their lavatories over the wall to the girls' lavatories – shouts which are clearly full of sexual innuendo (judging by the girls' responses) but equally clearly are about things the boys comprehend only very dimly!

Then there is the episode of Miss Flynn. There is a considerable element of prurience, or less than healthy sexual curiosity, in Laurie's attitude here. He has already indicated his awareness of her as an 'off-beat beauty', a 'pre-Raphaelite stunner'; he has indicated also how there was gossip about her, involving 'those fellows' which was hushed as soon as his pricked-up ears were noticed. In Fred Bates's description of how he found her body, the element to which Laurie's mind keeps returning is that 'she wasn't wearing a stitch of clothes': 'he'd seen drowned Miss Flynn with no clothes on'; 'She had come to it naked'. But, while his attitude is hardly commendable, it is also totally understandable and natural; for which of us has not at times wished to know the details of a grisly murder or attack? It is also true that out of the scene Lee creates a beautiful and evocative image of a drowned woman which is far from sexual.

There is a world of difference between a pre-adolescent boy's curiosity about sex and an adolescent boy's active interest in it. We see a good example of the first in the incidents with Jo. Laurie seems to approach her body with all the clinical lack of feeling of the doctor whom he is imitating. He is urged on essentially by inquisitiveness, a desire to know, rather than by any genuine sexual desire. Jo, too, seems to be at the same stage; and so they act out their ritual game, 'formal and grave'. There is a cool sterility in the exercise: the word 'cool' occurs in the episode, along with 'shivered' and the cold white images of 'candleskins' and 'something thrown down from the moon'.

This is definitely not a scene of passion.

The central episode with Rosie is clearly something different. Where Jo was cool, somewhat uncomprehending (though willing enough) and totally passive, Rosie Burdock is alluring, teasing, knowledgeable and eager, as can be seen from a few of the many phrases he uses of her: 'sly, glittering eyes'; 'cheap brass necklace'; 'bare legs . . . brown with hay-dust'; 'cat-like eyes and curling mouth'; 'her body seemed to flicker with lightning'; 'purring in the gloom'; 'her hair was rich as a wild bee's nest and her eyes were full of stings'; 'superbly assured'; 'perilous as quicksand'. Notice, however, that not only the girls are contrasted, but the settings also: where the one was darkening and chilly, the other is hot: 'a motionless day of summer, creamy, hazy, and amber-coloured'; 'her face was wrapped in a pulsating haze'. The cider is 'golden fire', 'wine of wild orchards, of russet summer . . . and Rosie's burning cheeks.'

And what of Laurie Lee in all this? The young boy so totally in charge of the situation with Jo, so scientific and objective in his explorations, is now a quivering mass of uncertainty, out of control and floundering: 'I was terrified of her'; 'I felt dry and dripping, icy hot'; 'I did not know what to do about her, nor did I know what not to do'; 'Skin drums beat in my head'; 'More fires were started'. Poor Laurie! (It goes without saying that this scene is a prime example of Lee willingly presenting himself in a slightly ridiculous light, laughing at his own ineptitude and inviting us to join in the laughter.) He has finally, then, reached the phase of sexual passion; new feelings have assaulted him; he is neither man nor boy, and things will never be the same again.

3.3 NOSTALGIA

Within this theme there are two distinct areas, perhaps not unconnected. The first is the nostalgia for the world of innocence which childhood is. It is almost inevitable that a middle-aged person looking back on his earliest years will view them with a wry shake of the head, perhaps hardly recognising in some respects the child he was then as the same human being he is now. And if one chooses to write about these years as Lee has done, then they must have evoked in him, as they do in us, a sense of loss. Because of Lee's remarkable ability to recreate his childhood mind, relating to us his feelings as if there had been no passing of the years, we feel even more acutely the naivety, the inexperience, the simplicity, the excited curiosity, the anticipation, which are so powerful in childhood.

At no time in the book, using his adult voice, does he write of his own childhood in sentimental terms; but then, as we have seen, he does not often present himself as the central focus. Every time he presents a child in a situation of wide-eyed innocence, however, he is in effect asking us to respond to the simplicity of youth: brother Tony in his make-believe world; Phyllis at his bedside with her hymns of Eden; Laurie himself thinking about the deserter, before he knew what war was – all of these are reminders of the short time in all our lives when life could be lived at a natural level, simple and free from care. But that innocence is part and parcel of a much wider innocence, the loss of which Lee felt acutely. More and more, as the book progresses, we see him viewing his youth as if it belonged to a totally different time, an age gone forever.

Consider for a moment the events which have so much changed the world of Slad since Laurie Lee was first set down there from the carrier's cart. On the global stage has been played out another World War, and this time Lee was old enough not just to understand but to take part. Shortly before that occurred the Spanish Civil War, which for Lee, as for many other writers and artists, was not just a war which, however tragic, had nothing to do with him – he was very much involved with it. The outside world has forced its way into every living-room, as radio, television and the press bring news almost before it has happened, and made so much entertainment 'canned' rather than home-based. The motor car and the aeroplane have transformed travel for the ordinary man; the Spain in which Laurie Lee was an almost solitary Briton in 1935 is now visited by six million people from Britain every year.

Much of this transformation, of course, can only be regarded as good news; Lee would certainly not wish us all to return to days of darkness and ignorance, to poor sanitation, to the 'welfare' of the Workhouse. What has been gained by 'progress', however, must be set against what has been lost, and it is about this loss that Lee is nostalgic. Basically, we have gained in scientific or technological terms, but have lost in human and social ones.

Consider first a very deep, and difficult, point, referred to briefly in the commentary on 'Public Death, Private Murder'. The relevant passage is on pp.104–5 of *Cider with Rosie*. What he writes of here is a kind of folk-memory, something intangible yet very real in the minds of the villagers. It is about 'our ghostly beginnings'; it is about the unchanged human life that had persisted in that valley 'since the Stone Age'. Yet change it did, in Lee's own lifetime. He managed to catch 'whiffs of something old as the glaciers', but 'That continuous contact has at last been broken'. Our very deepest roots have been cut off; roots which grew over countless generations. What we have left is only surface greenery. It is impossible to over-stress the importance of this idea in *Cider with Rosie* (and indeed outside it, too); Man's very nature, in the Slads of the world, has been drastically altered.

At more readily graspable human levels, we have lost much in the way of unsophisticated pleasure. The villagers Laurie Lee remembers were satisfied and contented with so much less than later generations demand. We see this in many ways: the simple games children played, summer and winter, with only the barest of 'props'; the joy his sisters took, either in dressing themselves up to go to see Granny Trill, or dressing the boys up too, for a Fancy Dress Parade; the excitement preceding the Annual Outing, which *all* the villagers except the vicar and squire joined in; the delight of rustic entertainment, presented by the villagers to the villagers; (notice, by the way, that the last three of these events happened only once, or once a year); the long walks for carol-singing; the testing of Granny Wallon's first wine of the season; the picnics; the walks with Mother – and so on. The infrequency of the 'treats' made them the sweeter; that so much was homespun and home-made only made it the more genuine and sincere.

Also readily understandable is the sense of community which existed in the village. Apart from events such as those just mentioned, in which the whole village participated, we can recognise other factors which promoted a strong feeling of 'belonging': all the children went to the same school, and were taught in only two classes – they knew each other from an early age; people rarely left the village for there was always work to be had, and the notion of 'mobility' had not really arrived (though it should be said that the First World War and even the Boer War had already begun to change things, as we see in 'The Uncles') – it was largely a static community; natural geographical features cut off Slad effectively in any case. It is not therefore surprising that we see many instances of the villagers being aware of each other in a very caring way: Mrs Lee, besides keeping a watchful eye on the Grannies, also called often on Miss Flynn; she popped in to see old Mr and Mrs Davies, and visited the Browns; the boys trooped up to Mr Wells's farm to see if he wanted any help in winter, or ran errands for Mrs Clissold; the girls dressed up to give Granny Trill a treat; the villagers talked in shocked tones of Miss Flynn's suicide: clearly all knew her well, 'different' though she was, and showed concern. (Incidentally, one should not be misled by the use of surnames by the villagers when speaking of, and to, each other: that more formal mode of address was perfectly normal.)

They could also close ranks on occasions, of course. The most controversial example of this is the refusal to identify for the police the youths who murdered the returning Vincent on that December night. Rather more palatable examples are the way in which they are drawn together as a unit once they are transported into unfamiliar territory on their annual outing: 'We began to look round fondly at our familiar selves, drawn close by this alien country. Waves of affection and loyalty embraced us'; or when Mr Crosby, the organist, was hysterical with stage-fright at the Annual Entertainment and desperate to get off: 'We loved him, however, and wouldn't let him go'. There is an enormous warmth of fellowship here which Lee feels has been lost with the break-up of village life as it was. However, Lee's nostalgia is mixed with the greatest good humour – even when describing the 'last days' of the village his tone is usually light; and this leads to the final part of this section.

3.4 LEE'S WORLD VIEW

This rather grandiose phrase is used here simply to indicate in general the way the writer looks at life in *Cider with Rosie*. First, his view is a very positive one. In serious literature there are very few writers whose normal tone is light; even among those whose view is essentially 'comic', the comedy is often harsh and cynical. But Laurie Lee derives enormous pleasure from the world. He finds much in human behaviour that is laughable, but his is never the laughter that mocks or belittles; moreover he is himself the most regular target when he points out the follies and absurdities of human behaviour. He also finds much that is quite simply 'good' in humanity; in the love, the care, the affection, the fellowship, the sharing, the giving, that was so much a part of his own family, but which he also saw in the village around him.

Next, he has a zest for living that will not be denied; its secret is in his insatiable curiosity about all things, whether he is prying into the endless variety of natural objects around him, or exploring another aspect of human behaviour and experience. Life is never grey in *Cider with Rosie*: winter brings its own sharp pleasures; death has its richness of emotion. In every way it is a good-humoured book, whose keynote is joy. He sees a positive life-force in every blade of grass; every day is a fresh awakening of the earth, and of him on it. (The anger which very rarely appears – but when it does, blazes rather than smoulders, as we might expect – is reserved for those who have stifled their own inner vitality, who seek to curb, to dampen, whose motto is 'Thou shalt not', who hide behind the cold blank wall of 'authority': 'visiting spinsters', magistrates, policemen, and some teachers. But such moments *are* rare.)

Such a view is in some sense religious, but it is not the religion of convention, the organised Church (his vicar is a poor specimen of humanity from Lee's viewpoint); rather it is a religion with older origins than Christianity: Harvest Festival, for him, was about a 'Church . . . older than its one foundation . . . as old as man's life on earth'; it is a religion with gods, spirits which inhabit the woods and fields; the religion which the earliest Christians found when they came to our shores, taking some of it over and giving it Christian significance. It is this which Lee feels he 'caught whiffs of' before it finally disappeared; (strangely enough, it is perhaps undergoing something of a revival now, as a backlash to twentieth-century values sets in.)

Remember, of course, that as a boy Laurie sang in the Church Choir, learned the Collects, went to Sunday School, sang carols, and so on; in other words, he was part of the orthodox church. He does not scorn this; many of his most profound experiences were in the quiet evenings at Evensong, for example. But there is something even older, something even beyond, which he has glimpsed only faintly, yet which seems to inspire his whole view of life's 'positive' nature. Even death is to be accepted with a 'frank and unfearful attitude', a natural partner to life, openly discussed, 'nobody tried to hide it'. There are times when a casual reader may even think him callous – 'Winter was the worst time for the old ones. Then they curled up like salted snails' – but such a thought shows misunderstanding: he sees death simply; it is the natural end to a natural process, and as such not evil, just natural.

A final word: there are ways in which *Cider with Rosie* is less an autobiography of Laurie Lee than a biography of his mother. Of course he mourns his mother; but this is a book not of mourning but of thanksgiving, a celebration of all those things with 'an edge of gold' which she saw, and taught him to see. 'I absorbed from birth, as now I know, the whole earth through her jaunty spirit.'

4 TECHNICAL FEATURES

4.1 LEE'S STYLE

As this word 'style' is one which frequently causes problems, it is as well to pause for a moment to examine what it means, in the context of writing. It is certainly not a word to be afraid of, or to be vague about. A writer's style is simply those characteristics in his writing which help us to identify a piece of work as his, even if we have not read it before. Most writers, whether of prose, poetry or drama, develop their own distinctive way of writing, and it is this which we call their 'style'.

In order to examine a style, we must of course analyse it, break it down as precisely as we can into its components, much as a forensic scientist would break down a chemical substance to determine, for instance, whether or not it contained any drugs, or alcohol, or poison. As it happens, Laurie Lee's style is so distinctive and individual that you would perhaps be able to recognise an unseen piece of his work already; but it is worth examining it in detail, picking out some of the ingredients which mingle to create it. (It should go without saying that there can be a considerable overlapping of these 'ingredients'; and also that, in taking a style apart, we should never lose sight of the whole, with all the parts reassembled.)

4.1.i Balancing word-patterns

Here are a few examples:

(a) from p.15 (He is writing about washing-days): 'soapsuds boiling, bellying and popping, creaking and whispering, rainbowed with light and winking with a million windows'; (balance of -ing words and pairs of images);

(b) from p.25 (inside the cottage): 'together with an infinite range of objects that folded, fastened, creaked and sighed, opened and shut, tinkled and sang, pinched, scratched, cut, burned, spun, toppled, or fell to pieces';

(c) from p.133 (about his mother): 'Her flowers and songs, her unshaken fidelities, her attempts at order, her relapses into squalor, her near madness, her crying for light, her almost daily weeping for her dead child-daughter, her frisks and gaieties, her fits of screams, her love of man, her hysterical rages, her justice towards each of us children';

(d) from p.116 (again about his mother): 'Mischievous, muddle-headed, full of brilliant fancies, half witless, half touched with wonder';

(e) from p.152: 'Summer was also the time of these: of sudden plenty, of slow hours and actions, of diamond haze and dust on the eyes, of the valley in post-vernal slumber; of burying birds out of seething corruption; of Mother sleeping heavily at noon; of jazzing wasps and dragonflies, haystooks and thistle-seeds, snows of white butterflies, skylarks' eggs, bee-orchids, and frantic ants; of wolf-cub parades, and boy scouts' bugles; of sweat running down the legs; of boiling potatoes on bramble fires, of flames glass-blue in the sun; of lying naked in the hill-cold stream.'

(This is little more than half of this particular 'list'.) What is gained by such piling-up of images? Principally a great feeling of richness in the language, for the less meaningful elements in a sentence pattern can be missed out. (Look at example 'd' above. Lee might have written: 'My mother was a very mischievous girl, and at times muddle-headed too, though she was full of brilliant fancies', but how thinly spread the meaning would have become, compared with the solid lumps of Lee's phrases.) Also gained is a sense of the teeming abundance of life itself, and the gloriously varied richness of all human experience.

A similar feature to this 'listing' is the way in which he regularly groups his images, phrases or words in threes; this is a fairly common practice, but nevertheless noticeable: 'squat, hard-hitting, heavy-drinking heroes'; 'to the fall of a coal, the sneeze of a cat, or a muted exclamation'; 'his curious, crooked, suffering face'; 'then we filed into the stalls, took our privileged places, and studied the congregation;' 'the houses, the halls, the places of paradise had all been visited.'

4.1.ii **The prose-poetry of Lee's writing**

It is this more than anything else that is his distinguishing feature. What do I mean by the phrase prose–poetry? Simply this: that *Cider with Rosie*, though written in the normal structures of prose, has many of the qualities and devices more usually associated with poetry. These qualities and devices may be divided into three groups.

(i) *Simile, metaphor, alliteration and onomatopoeia*

Here are a few examples of these, culled from all over the book.

(a) 'one was boarded by them, bussed and buttoned, or swung up high like a wriggling fish to be hooked and held in their lacy linen.' (Examples of alliteration and assonance are underlined.)
(b) 'The light came through her nightdress like sand through a sieve.' (Notice in this simile how, as well as the notion of 'filtering' conveyed by the comparison, there is also the added idea of a pleasurable tactile sensation: sand running through the fingers.)
(c) 'Bees blew like cake-crumbs . . . white butterflies like sugared wafers.' (As well as the alliteration, and the comparison by colour – unusual though the choice is – there is an image of the sweetness of valley life in 'cakes' and 'sugared wafers'. A good simile will strike the reader because the comparison is fresh and unusual; but also will add some other quality besides just a literal similarity.)
(d) 'She is a coil of smoke, a giggling splutter, a reek of cordite.' (This metaphor about his sister Dorothy effectively captures the essence of her character - she is explosive and volatile, like the firework he is here referring to.)
(e) 'Like cold twin stars, linked but divided, they survived by a mutual balance.' (This is a brilliant choice of simile for the two grannies, for their hostility joins as well as separates them; and what could be more chilling than a remote star in its desolate isolation?)
(f) Fred Bates 'was a thin, scrubby lad with a head like a bottle brush.'
(g) His uncles 'like a ring of squat megaliths on some local hill, bruised by weather and scarred with old glories' – a splendid picture of these seemingly indestructible men.
(h) 'He moved with stiff and stilted strides, swinging his silvered beard'.
(i) 'soapsuds boiling, bellying and popping, creaking and whispering . . . bubble bubble . . . rinsing and slapping . . . panting'. (This example of onomotopoeia – that is, the use of words whose sound

echoes their meaning – provides a clear illustration of how thick is the texture of Lee's language; how many jobs it does at the same time; how rich it is because of the concentration of meaning.)

There is also a very good example of extended metaphor on pp.13–15. The handful of examples given above could easily have been multiplied fifty times over, so full is the text of such qualities.

(ii) *The very careful choice of vocabulary*

In particular there is the use of words which are unusual in their contexts. In all areas of life, the unusual attracts attention. Sometimes, however, the attracting of attention is the sole aim of being unusual; in such cases, what is unusual will not be worthy of study, since its aim is entirely self-centred: the equivalent of a child shouting, 'Look at me!' When a writer (or speaker, though this happens less often) uses language in an unusual way, he is of course wanting to stop us in our tracks, but he always has a point – to make us look more closely; even, at times, to make us really wrestle with his words, until they yield their fullest meaning.

In *Cider with Rosie* Lee rarely makes searching demands on his readers; but at the same time his love of life includes a great love of language, and he clearly enjoys playing with words, poking them around, stretching and squeezing them; in general getting as much from them as he possibly can. No doubt he owed much of this enjoyment and skill to his mother, who 'would make up snap verses about local characters that could stab like a three-pronged fork.' Here, first, are one or two simple examples.

(a) On p.114 Lee describes his mother 'sketching the landscape in a delicate snowflake scribble'. The word 'delicate' is a fairly obvious one to describe her lightness of touch, but 'snowflake' is a startling choice. It is a splendid choice, too, however, for it conjures up qualities that are at the heart of Laurie Lee's mother: her airy lightness, the half-hold that she has on reality (just as the snowflake falls and melts away), the apparently aimless drifting of its fall, the gentle beauty.

(b) This time a blank space replaces one of Lee's words. Write down half a dozen words that could fill the gap. Lee is writing about Joseph and Hannah Brown: 'They did nothing more than was necessary to live, but did it fondly, with skill – they sat together in their . . . kitchen enjoying their half-century of silence.' What have you suggested? 'Cosy', 'warm', 'peaceful' are possible choices, but

Lee's word is 'clock-ticking'. Again there is the two-fold reaction. First we are brought up sharp by the unusual word; then we stop to think about it. Here are two old people who are as much in love with each other as in their youth – indeed more. Just to be together is all they need; words are superfluous in the gentle peace of their evenings. Softly measuring out the hours is the quiet tick of the clock. It is a symbol of their own steadiness, their own fifty years of life together.

(c) This next is a more difficult example. In Infant School, Laurie is 'idling voluptuously through the milky days with a new young teacher to feed on.' The two underlined parts are of course connected: Lee has described how his days in the Infant School were days of innocence; milk is the food of all mammal babies, therefore his image is one in which his young teacher becomes a mother-substitute for the young boy. But it goes further than this, for there is also the growing sexual awareness of the boy, and the notion of a mother feeding a baby to Laurie Lee in the 1920s is clearly one of breast-feeding; so the image contains an element in which he is aware of the soft feminine roundness of his young teacher, as he had been of his own mother in the memorable passage where he describes sleeping in her bed when he was very young. The clinching factors – if one needs them – are his use of the word 'voluptuously' in the same sentence: a word full of sensuous awareness; and the description earlier of his young teacher 'leaning her bosom against our faces, and guiding our wandering fingers'.

(d) He is writing of the deaths of Miss Flynn and Vincent: 'the sharp death-taste, *tooth-edge* of violence, the yielding to the water of that despairing beauty, the *indignant* blood in the snow.' The murder of Vincent was a savage, brutal affair. It is as if his red blood itself is a cry of outrage and indignation, starkly staining the winter whiteness. 'Tooth-edge' carries with it all the ferocity of the beast of prey, its fangs honed for the tearing of flesh. A snarling guard-dog, lip curled back, teeth bared: this is the image Lee is creating. It is just possible that both words are pointers, too, to Lee's own reaction to the murder, filled with protest and horror as they are.

(iii) *Imagery*

The third quality in the 'prose-poetry' of Lee's writing is the remarkably rich, sensuous imagery he uses, by which is meant the way he is constantly evoking all five of our senses – sight, sound, touch, taste, smell. For Lee, as was pointed out in the commentary on Section 7, 'Life is rich, life is full; everything it brings, every sight and sound, every experience, is to be savoured, sucked, milked until its essence is part of him.' This impression is conveyed to us mainly through the sensuous imagery which abounds, tumbling over itself like an over-loaded applecart. Entering *Cider with Rosie* is like walking off the street into one of those wonderful continental covered markets; you are met with a din to rival Bedlam as seething sellers and buyers call out their wares and wishes; the eye struggles to take in the myriads of colours of food of all kinds, from silver-scaled fish to olive-green water-melons; the air is heady as the tang of lemon meets the sweet ripeness of peaches; each newly encountered smell brings a corresponding taste, and all seems like chaos.

Here are three fairly short and typical passages which explore this sensuousness.

(a) The first is full of 'taste' images, and requires no comment: 'one nibbled one's way like a rat through roots and leaves. Peas rolled under the tongue, fresh cold, like solid water; teeth chewed green peel of apples, acid sharp, and the sweet white starch of swedes. Beaten away by wet hands gloved with flour, one returned in a morose and speechless lust. Slivers of raw pastry, moulded, warm, went down in the shapes of men and women – heads and arms of unsalted flesh seasoned with nothing but a dream of cannibalism.'

(b) The second is full of images of touch, the wonderful warmth (of love as well as body heat) which the young Laurie feels in his mother's bed: 'So in the ample night and the thickness of her hair I consumed my fattened sleep, drowsed and nuzzling to her warmth of flesh, blessed by her bed and safety. From the width of the house and the separation of the day, we two then lay joined alone. The darkness to me was like the fruit of sloes, heavy and ripe to the touch . . . In her flights of dream she held me close, like a parachute to her back; or rolled and enclosed me with her great tired body so that I was snug as a mouse in a hayrick.' This, again, requires no comment.

(c) The third is a rich mixture of touch, smell, sound and taste, with a dazzlingly colourful series of sight images too: 'Small heated winds blew over our faces, dandelion seeds floated by, burnt sap and roast nettles tingled our nostrils together with the dull rust smell of dry ground. The grass was June high and had come up with a rush, a massed entanglement of species, crested with flowers and spears of wild wheat, and coiled with clambering vetches, the whole of it humming with blundering bees and flickering with scarlet butterflies. Chewing grass on our backs, the grass scaffolding the sky, the summer was all we heard; cuckoos crossed distances on chains of cries, flies buzzed and choked in the ears, and the saw-toothed chatter of mowing-machines drifted on waves of air from the fields.'

It is not necessary to draw up a list of 'what he could see,' 'what he could hear' and so on, though it would be a useful exercise. What should be noticed however, is how almost every noun – the basic element in the sentence – is enriched by an adjective: 'small, heated winds', 'burnt sap', 'roast nettles', 'dull rust smell', 'blundering bees', 'scarlet butterflies', and so on. Notice, too, the vivid onomatopoeic words, 'humming', 'flickering', 'buzzed', 'chatter'; and the sheer variety of sensuous experience that is taking place, as well as the variety within each sense – the different types of sound he hears, for example. Yet this passage is little more than a hundred words long!

The effect of such vivid and rich imagery is to make the writing, and the mental picture it creates, three-dimensional. One final point is worthy of attention because it concerns both the style and the effect created by a passage such as this. The words that carry the meaning in language, the words that conjure up images, are nouns, verbs, adjectives and (to a lesser extent) adverbs; the others (prepositions, conjunctions, articles, and so on) supply the connections. To put that idea into concrete terms, words such as 'sand', 'wasp', 'fled', 'exhausted', 'grim', 'flattened', convey a clearer picture than 'of', 'by', 'the', 'after', 'when', or 'or'. Therefore the more of the first type of word a writer uses, proportionately, the 'thicker' or 'denser' is the picture he creates. Because Lee, as we have just seen, fills his work with adjectives; because, as we saw earlier, he misses out the 'connectors' by piling up lists; and because, so often, the words he chooses are words to be mulled over and savoured, so the meaningful words in his writing are thicker on the ground, and their sense rich and heavy.

4.1.iii His economy

It is interesting to note that, while much of his writing bursts at the seams, so crammed is it with imagery, as we have just seen, nevertheless at times Lee can be very economical in his use of words. On such occasions, he condenses what he has to say into the simplest and plainest of statements. Here are a few examples:

(a)
'. . . gazing in silence at the gardens'. This, from p.25, describes the men of the village who have just returned from the First

World War. In these few words are contained so much of the horror of that war; the men 'gaze' – a static, frozen stare – 'in silence' (as if what they have undergone has made them dumb) 'at the gardens' – which, in the mud of France, they thought they would never see again. There is a numbness, a dumbness, a shell-shock in their lifeless posture, and a pathos in the notion of a garden and all it symbolises of colour, growth and peace.

(b) Hannah and Joseph Brown 'did not see each other again, for in a week they both were dead.' To appreciate this particular example fully, it is necessary to reread the whole episode, from 'But if you survived' (p.108). The Browns' story is heartbreakingly emotional, and Lee unashamedly wrings every last drop from it; yet here, at the very end, the stark, bare statement says it all.

(c) There is a similar example at the very end of the section 'Mother', on p.135. After Laurie's father died, 'she never mentioned him again, but spoke to shades, saw visions, and then she died. We buried her in the village, under the edge of the beechwood, not far from her four-year-old daughter.' This is very plain writing, yet the emotional depth is all the more profound because of it. The pen is controlled, perhaps because, in these intensely personal circumstances, Lee would not have trusted himself to cope with unreined feelings.

(d) An example of a different kind, from p.121, about his father and mother: 'So she fell in love with him immediately, and remained in love for ever. And herself being comely, sensitive, and adoring, she attracted my father also. And so he married her. And so later he left her – with his children and some more of her own.'

The economy here has a different cause, perhaps: Lee avoids writing anything of his father; though he was three when he came to Slad, he says 'I don't know where I lived before then.' In particular he seems not to wish to dwell on those few years of happiness which his mother shared with his father. The abrupt statements, 'And so he married her. And so later he left her' are so absurdly lacking in emotion as to suggest a callousness in the actions themselves.

(e) Finally, an indication of how economy can be used to humorous effect, too. This time, the piled up events are mentioned so casually that it is as though it is all in a day's work for a young lad. Laurie is visiting Uncle Charlie and his children:

'Then we play with their ferrets, spit down their well, have a fight, and break down a wall. Later we are called for and given a beating, then we climb up the tree by the earth closet. Edie climbs highest, till we bite her legs, then she hangs upside down and screams. It has been a full, far-flung, and satisfactory day; dusk falls and we say good-bye.'

4.1.iv His variety of tone

In a book which is so much a celebration of the joy of life, it will be clear that *lightness* is the normal tone of Lee's writing – this is writing with a smile on its face. Examples can be found all over the book; one of them, which you may reread, is the description of 'Crabby', Laurie's first headteacher, in the second and third paragraphs on p.49.

However, there is much *nostalgia* in *Cider with Rosie*, too, which introduces a much sadder note. A good example of this is when Lee writes of his mother talking about her husband, on p.122, from 'Take out your pins' to 'his favourites then.' This is, in fact, doubly nostalgic, for Lee is writing nostalgically about his mother, who in turn is reminiscing nostalgically about her husband.

He is also a master of *pathos*, the feeling that springs from helplessness (either the helplessness of the victim, or our own helplessness in being unable to do anything). The best illustration of this is probably the death of his sister, Frances, on p.157. The details which create the pathos are her youth – she was only four; her fragile beauty; her nursing of her baby brother; her 'baby-talk' to him, as if he and she occupied a world of their own; and her uncomplaining death, 'in a chair in the corner of the room'.

Only rarely is there *a stern element* in his writing, but it does show at times, and powerfully; in recounting how the 'authorities' killed off Joseph and Hannah Brown, for example (pp.110–111); or, in similar vein, in attacking the authorities and the law (pp.205–6); perhaps, too, in his remark on p.57 against society in general for condemning children for the accident of birth that made them the offspring of an incestuous partnership. Still less often is there any trace of *bitterness*, though perhaps his description of his father on p.61 (from 'He was a natural fixer' to 'scarcely missed him') contains that deep and destructive feeling.

Much more in his line is *compassion*, for Lee is ever ready to feel for those whose lot in life is hard, especially if the hardship is caused through no fault of their own. Thus, for instance, his caring sympathy for the old is clear – the two grannies, the Browns, Mr and Mrs Davies, his own mother; and at the other end of the scale, those young children born into poverty or social disfavour excite his sympathy. A good example of this is seen on pp.57–8. The gipsy boy at school, Rosso, was at first mistrusted and ostracized by the other children. But one day, almost literally starving, he stole some food, was caught by the teacher, severely beaten, and then ran home. Lee pictures the miserable hovel the boy returns to – an encampment in the mud of the quarry – and is half-ashamed of his own comparative luxury. 'Gipsies no longer seemed either sinister or strange.' The word 'compassion' literally means 'suffering along with'; that is exactly what young Laurie was doing.

Most of the time the tone is clear enough in *Cider with Rosie*; nevertheless it is necessary to remain on guard for slight (or even considerable) changes of tone, for Lee is a writer whose words are chosen with great skill and care, as we have seen.

4.1.v His humour

In some ways the matter of Lee's humour should have been included in the previous section, as his tone is very often humorous. As humour is notoriously difficult to discuss, no attempt will be made to point out why any particular passage is comic. Nevertheless, it is worthwhile trying to analyse the book's humour, putting different types into separate compartments.

(a) Stock situation

First, some of his comedy depends upon a situation, ofen a 'stock' situation – that is, the kind of situation from which comedy is so often created that we can almost anticipate it. For instance, the Parochial Church Tea and Annual Entertainment in which Major Doveton falls foul of his banjo, Mrs Pimbury sings two odd songs, and finally the Baroness von Hodenburg renders a Germanic folk-song of her own making, is typical of the stock situation. Or consider the passage in which Uncle Tom is chased, literally, by the monstrous Effie Mansell, a six-footer determined to 'get her man'. There is too a delightful passage (pp.224–5) in which the Lee family put on all manner of shy and unnatural politenesses when Marjorie first brings a boy home.

Lee is also a supreme master in telling a comical story. The best example of this, which you should reread for yourselves, is the episode on pp.50–1 in which Spadge Hopkins, the biggest boy in the school, has finally had enough of Crabby and, after a brief struggle, picks her up and sets her on top of the classroom cupboard. (It should be added that this is hardly – one hopes – a stock situation!)

A last example is the behaviour of the girls when Jones's goat walks up the street, on pp.30–1, ending with 'Phyl didn't answer: she had run away, and was having hysterics in the pantry.'

(b) *Straight-faced humour*

Very different is the kind of remark Lee makes without preparing us for it. If you do not have your wits about you, it is very easy to miss this type of humour. One very good example of this occurs when the boys are carol-singing. Boney keeps singing flat. 'The others forbade him to sing it at all, and Boney said he would fight us. Picking himself up, he agreed we were right'. (The reader is required to provide the missing 'action'.)

Another example concerns Uncle Sid's bus-driving: he caused havoc, but 'always took pains to avoid women and children and scarcely ever mounted the pavements.' Later, still with Uncle Sid: when he was suspended with pay, 'out of respect for Aunt Alice, he always committed suicide. Indeed he committed suicide more than any man I know, but always in the most reasonable manner.'

Another: the valley 'was not high and open like the Windrush country, but had secret origins, having been gouged from the Escarpment by the melting ice-caps some time before we got there.' And finally, the boys are in a stable planning the Brith Wood rape: 'We drew closer together, out of earshot of the horse.'

(c) *Naivety*

Especially in the early part of the book we find Lee making comedy out of his childish misconceptions.

Because the deserter who used to come to their house sometimes was hiding in the wood, for instance, Laurie thought that was where the war must be. 'I imagined him sleeping, then having a go at the battle, then coming down to us for a cup of tea.' There is more than a touch of pathos in this, too, of course, for the innocent child is totally unaware of the grisly reality of the First World War.

We see this elsewhere: having been told that his uncles were 'in the war' he wonders, now the war is over 'what would happen to my uncles who lived in it?'. His confusing of his father with the Kaiser is likewise naive and pathetic though with perhaps a hint of malicious humour, too, in view of Lee's attitude to his father. Finally, he pokes fun at his own childish gullibility about the curse laid on those who talked about seeing the Bulls Cross Coach: 'a curse we all believed in – you went white in the night, and your teeth fell out, and later you died by trampling.'

(d) *Word-play*

It is not surprising that Lee, who is so fond of words and loves
experimenting with them, should occasionally take delight in creating
humour by twisting the senses of words, or by producing an unexpected image. (Much comedy, after all, depends on the unexpected.)
Here are a few examples, without comment:

> Water 'would drip all day from clouds and trees, from roofs and
> eaves and noses.'
> [I could] 'subtract certain numbers from each other. I had even
> just succeeded in subtracting Poppy from Jo'.
> 'Miss B, the Head Teacher, to whom I was now delivered,
> being about as physically soothing as a rake.'
> 'It was lentil-stew usually, a heavy brown mash made appa-
> rently of plastic studs.'
> 'I can never read a Collect today without tasting a crisp burnt
> sausage'.

There are other kinds of humour, too, in much smaller doses: a very
fine piece of *irony*, for instance, when he tells what happened to some
of his young friends in their later lives (p.215); and a neat touch of
pathos with humour in telling us that, on her death, Granny Trill left
'nothing on the air . . . but the tiniest cloud of snuff.'

One final point is worth making: Lee's humour is never cruel or
wounding; rarely if at all is there sarcasm or any form of malicious-
ness; indeed it is not often that he takes human beings as his targets.
If he is apt to smile sometimes at the foibles of humanity, he does so
not as a cynical observer – as if he himself belonged to another
species – but rather as a man who recognises his own foolishness in
the foolishness of others, and can laugh heartily at himself.

4.1.vi Literary references and allusions

This is a minor point, but one perhaps worth a brief mention. Lee
occasionally uses a phrase taken consciously or otherwise from
another writer. The problem about this, of course, is that, while one
can detect a few such allusions, one will almost certainly have missed
at least as many more. Another reader could well find others. Many
writers use 'borrowed' phrases in this way; indeed any educated
person does; but it is a factor, though a tiny one, in Lee's overall

style. Here are a few of these allusions, and the writers they are taken from:

    'piping loud' – William Blake
    'the nightfall of that first day' – the Bible (Genesis)
    'time hung golden and suspended' – Dylan Thomas
    'my mounting strength of days' – Dylan Thomas
    'that green age' – Dylan Thomas
    'a local habitation not fit to be named' – Shakespeare
    'our tiring-houses' – Shakespeare

(Some of Dylan Thomas's work is suggested in the Further Reading section, as possibly no writer's style is as close to Lee's as his.)

4.2 LEE AS A NARRATOR

It is worth reminding ourselves at the outset that *Cider with Rosie* is not a novel. Many of the narrative elements which one looks for in the novelist, therefore, one will not find here: in particular the creation of imaginative incident; the skilful working-out of a plot; the weaving together of different strands of the tale; the standpoint adopted by the writer – is he a character in the story or does he tell it in the third person; does he tell the story in flashback, or in 'logical' time? Yet it is possible, and I think necessary, to examine Lee's narrative strengths, for he *is* telling a story, though not writing a novel, and within *Cider with Rosie* are many complete incidents, told in narrative fashion.

In looking first at the *structure* of this book, we can see easily enough that there is a loose chronology about it, but only a loose one. The opening section, 'First Light', deals with some of Lee's earliest recollections of his arrival in Slad; while the final section, 'Last Days', looks back on the changes that overtook the village, and the breaking up of the Lee household. Even within the first section, however, Lee is already writing with hindsight in his 'adult' voice, while the last section takes the reader way beyond the fifteen-year-old boy to the mature philosophies of a middle-aged writer.

Many of the sections deal with incidents culled from any part of his first fifteen years – and after. Indeed, apart from the first three sections of the book, there is little attempt to establish a time-scale. We can divide the book into five sub-sections:

(i) sections 1 to 3: these take us more or less chronologically through Laurie Lee's life from the age of three until he leaves school;

(ii) sections 4 to 6: these extend the book's world from a preoccupa-
      tion with the Lee family and Laurie himself to the wider area
      outside – from 'The Kitchen' to 'The Grannies in the Wainscot'
      to the events of the village in 'Public Death, Private Murder';
(iii) section 7: the central section, dealing solely with the life-history
      of Mother Lee;
(iv) sections 8 to 12: each of these takes a single theme and
      elaborates on it, regardless of time, though 'First Bite at the
      Apple' inevitably deals with the early teenage years;
(v)   section 13: in large part, an objective looking-back at the end of
      the 'old' village and the end of the family unit in the cottage.

Next, a look at Lee as a story-teller, for *Cider with Rosie* abounds in
episodes which are complete tales in themselves. To suggest a few at
random: the outing to Weston-super-Mare; the death of Miss Flynn;
the Brith Wood rape; the murder of Vincent; Jones's goat; the
carol-singing; his experiments with Jo; the Annual Entertainment;
the Browns; his mother's history; cider with Rosie. An analysis of
just one of these episodes – the death of Miss Flynn – will illustrate
Lee's narrative skills. (The passage is from p.98: 'Grief or madness . . .' to p.104; 'drowned in that pond.'

For Lee, the story is not to be told for 'suspense'; he tells us from
the first that it was a suicide; the question is rather one of circumstances and motivation. He also hints from the beginning at
'madness' being an underlying cause. To this is added, at the very
start, the very powerful image of the dead woman (though he saw her
corpse only in his imagination) which 'remains with me till this day.'
Within a paragraph, then, our curiosity is roused: it is a suicide, there
are 'lowered voices', she was strange but beautiful, a solitary woman,
and the story is still powerful in Lee's mind.

He then describes Miss Flynn: tall, pale, a 'stunning' woman, but
odd. (At this stage we must remind ourselves that Laurie was very
young at this time, and that there were things said about Miss Flynn
that were not considered fit for little boys to hear. He grasped this
intuitively, as children do.) The hints about Miss Flynn are subtle,
and pervade the story, but are never conclusively clarified. Laurie's
mother says: 'There are others more wicked, poor soul.' ('Wicked' in
what way?)

After a further description of her witch-like attraction, Lee recalls
the last occasion the boys and their mother saw her. With his acute
eye for detail, he tells us she 'stared down at her hands' and 'lifted
one knee and pointed her toe' – not eccentric gestures so much as a
sign of her internal conflicts – before she confesses that she has 'been

bad for the things I must do.' Her mother's sick spirit has been tormenting her. Notice, however, that her language is as full of riddles as the woman herself. Does 'bad' mean 'ill' or 'wicked'? Are 'things I must do' things she has felt compelled to do, in the past, or things she will be compelled to do, in the future – kill herself, for instance? (There are hints that she is 'wicked' elsewhere in this passage.)

Lee's mother throws out another unexplained fact – 'and she half-gentry, too.' Was Miss Flynn one of the all-too-frequent products of an affair between a local landowner and a country girl, a poor creature with one foot in each world but belonging to neither?

Then comes a brief time-lapse before the Sunday morning, when Fred Bates was late with the milk. Even though we know what Miss Flynn's fate was to be, Lee manages to keep us waiting, suspensefully, until Fred tells his tale. It is his account which works on young Laurie's imagination: the white figure, her nakedness, her staring eyes under the water.

The story at this point has a very sharp edge, composed of many elements, all beautifully combined and kept under control: most noticeable is the honesty with which Lee analyses his and the girls' response; Miss Flynn's death did not occasion grief, but wonder, excitement, bright-eyed scandal and prurience ('he'd seen drowned Miss Flynn with no clothes on.') This is the natural human response to such an event in any community, and we are now given the conversations of anonymous villagers as they talk about the news.

Their conversations reveal Lee's excellent ear for dialogue; he captures exactly the way people talk when they are on close terms with each other. These speakers also supply further hints about Miss Flynn – something to do with men, but more than that – but Laurie, spotted listening, runs off, and he (and we) learn no more. Excitement and dread take him to the pond (where other villagers, typically, have also gone). Laurie hoped not to be seen (a sense of shame; an intrusion on Miss Flynn's privacy, even though she is dead, and her body gone?) Then he looks into the water and recreates the suicide in a most beautiful simile: 'She had come to it naked, alone in the night, and had slipped into it like a bed; she lay down there, and drew the water over her, and drowned quietly away in the reeds.' The picture is overpoweringly real, in his mind and ours; Miss Flynn in memory is forever 'drowned in that pond'.

Lee's strengths here, then, are his swift but telling characterisation (we know all we need to know of Miss Flynn from a handful of words); his realistic portrayal of human responses to particular situations; his ear for dialogue, and keen sense of when to use it; his evocative, sensuous description; his ability to make his readers see and feel as vividly as he does; and the subtlety with which he unfolds a situation. Other episodes in the book would, of course, reveal additional qualities in his narration – in particular, the ability to 'shape' a story, giving it a satisfying completeness.

4.3 THE PEOPLE IN THE BOOK

I have deliberately chosen the word 'people' rather than 'characters' as a reminder that we are not dealing with a work of fiction, with invented characters, but with the real world of the living, and the dead. Lee's book contains far too many people to permit a close look at all of them here. Accordingly this book will examine his immediate family only, beginning however with the central figure we can easily pass by as he presents himself in *Cider with Rosie*.

4.3.i The author himself

There is a problem here, of course, for though Laurie Lee attains the age of fourteen or fifteen in the book, he is writing it in his forties. In fact, we learn much more, inevitably, about the man than about the boy. Human beings rarely change fundamentally, however and, except where clearly adult notions arise, there is no need to attempt to separate the young lad within the book from the grown man writing it.

There is a pertinent and very interesting passage in another book of Lee's *I Can't Stay Long*. In the chapter called 'Writing Autobiography' he has this to say about the writing of *Cider with Rosie*: 'I was less interested, anyway, in giving a portrait of myself, than in recording the details of that small local world . . . It seemed to me that my own story would keep.' Of *Cider with Rosie* after the first three chapters he writes: 'Then the book moved away from me . . . I became at this stage less a character than a presence, a listening shadow, a moving finger.' Only in the section 'Sick Boy' does Lee concentrate on an aspect of himself; yet though he is for much of *Cider with Rosie* 'less a character than a presence' there is quite a lot to be gleaned about his character in the book.

The first thing to be said – and it should be stressed – is that Laurie Lee was a perfectly normal boy. He had perhaps more than his fair share of illness, but this made him neither a weakling nor a hypochondriac. He is accepted by the other village boys as 'one of the gang' and joins in such activities as a violent game of cricket (at

Sixpence Robinson's); sliding around on the ice when Jones's pond froze over; a game of 'Fox and Hounds' in the quiet darkness of the summer countryside, and so on. We also read of the tremendous delight he takes in the vigorous physical prowess of his uncles. He seeks out horrors, too, whether in the garden or on the pier at Weston.

This quality has been placed first because there is perhaps a tendency to equate great sensitivity with a lack of robustness; such an equation simply does not hold true in Laurie's case, nor, one suspects, in general. Nevertheless he was a very sensitive boy. This is hardly surprising, given his circumstances, for the strongest formative influences on his childhood were all female – his mother and older sisters. It is worth remembering, too, how susceptible his home life made him to family influences; eight people lived in their cottage, most of the time in the kitchen; there was much less 'going out', as entertainment was only to be found in the towns; and the 'canned' entertainment of radio and television had not yet arrived. The family 'trod on each other like birds in a hole.' There has been discussion elsewhere, in section commentaries, of the debt he owed to his mother in particular; much of that debt was in the area of sensitivity and awareness.

Much of it, too, was to do with enthusiasm and zest for living. He wants to sample all manner of human experience, learning from it something more about the human condition. It is this capacity to enjoy which is probably his most noticeable characteristic. Along with this capacity we find several closely related ones. He has a very highly developed sense of humour, for instance – a topic touched on earlier in this section. But his humour is not malicious.

Lee also has great compassion for, and understanding of, most of the rest of humanity, especially that part of it which makes up the great mass of ordinary people; and among these he reserves his strongest feelings for the helpless young and the equally helpless old. It is in this connection that we see his rare flashes of anger against that cold voice of authority whose victims are so often the old or the young. He has a deep mistrust of those who are 'outside' yet interfere; who reduce human beings to numbers; who take away the individuality, the uniqueness which is everyone's birthright, and lay on all the dead hand of bureaucracy and conformity. Throughout the book, no authority figure emerges with credit; from 'Crabby B' to the vicar; from magistrates and police to the 'Visiting Spinsters' who took away and separated the Browns: all are seen as either fools, hypocrites or tyrants. Such moments are very rare in *Cider with Rosie* but perhaps all the more memorable because of their rarity.

The other side of that particular trait is what seems to be an innate belief in the essential common sense of humanity; people in general are to be entrusted with their own destinies; communities will themselves, without outside promptings, create and enforce their own acceptable standards of decency and morality. There seems to be an obvious connection between such a belief and the nature of the Lee family: brought up amidst so much genuine love, affection and caring, how could Laurie Lee have felt other than that there is a basic goodness at the heart of humanity?

Lee admits that, at school, he showed little academic flair, compared with his brother Jack, for instance. He was, in his own delightful phrase, a natural Infant. Two things are noticeable here, however. Firstly, it is hardly surprising that the young boy we see in this book, with a boundless, bursting-out joy in life, a love of colour and light and glorious chaos, should find the strictures of school unbearable. (Certain it is that many of his occupations in later life could not have been undertaken without a very high level of intelligence.)

The second point is this: he has a very self-effacing character. In most works of autobiography the figure of the writer is constantly centre-stage; indeed, if one stops to consider the reasons why any man would write his autobiography, one will probably conclude that a strong belief in his own self-importance ranks high in the list. Yet somehow this never seems to be the case with *Cider with Rosie*. Bearing in mind the words from *I Can't Stay Long*, quoted earlier, I feel that Lee was writing a biography of his mother rather than an autobiography – and in addition to 'recording the details of that small local world'. Illustrations of this self-effacement are not hard to find: in almost every situation he presents himself as inadequate, foolish, or naive – the very first picture we are given is of the three-year-old Laurie howling because he has been left alone, and almost the last is of his inexpert fumblings with Rosie and his humiliation (along with the 'gang') by Lizzy Berkeley. Moreover, those things which he clearly does well are made little of: his poetry writing is hardly mentioned, nor is his fiddle-playing – even though this latter became his sole source of income on his first Spanish journey.

Finally, he is that very rare person who is both an observer of life yet at the same time a willing participant; who has the sharpest of eyes for human folly yet is free from cynicism; who has a very powerful inner life, yet also wears his inner life on the outside, for all to see; who, above all, has a boundless curiosity about life in all its enthralling variety, and an unquenchable thirst for the wine of experience.

4.3.ii His sisters

There are many episodes in the book in which the three girls are
practically indistinguishable, where he lumps them together in affection: 'How magnificent they appeared, full-rigged, those towering
girls, with their flying hair and billowing blouses'; 'The girls squirmed
in their chairs and began giggling horribly; they appeared to have
gone off their heads'. Or occasionally Lee's memory will seem to fail
him in so far as he cannot remember which of the three said or did
this or that; ('seem' because there are times when perhaps the
'forgetting' is deliberate, as when he does not identify which sister,
with her boyfriend, created the family row (p.228) – the only point in
the book where one sees the members of the household at violent
loggerheads.) However, though memory has fused three girls into
one at times, a close reading shows them to be very separate and
individual.

Marjorie

Marjorie was, of course, the oldest of the family. Perhaps the phrase
which best sums her up is 'a natural mother' (p.62). When Laurie's
eyes were bunged up, it was for Marjorie that he called; she it was
who stuffed him with currants on their first arrival at the cottage; she
it was who took charge when their mother went away for a few days.
The love Marjorie feels for the younger children is everywhere
apparent: she sits in vigil at Laurie's bedside when he is very ill; she is
worried about leaving the children alone in the house the night the
war ends – indeed she will not do it. She radiates caring as a nurse
does.

She was a beautiful girl in the conventional sense, but even more
beautiful because her inner grace shone through her, too; slow,
dreamy, quite unconscious of self, placid, contented, Marjorie, like
her sisters, was 'not hard to admire'; in Lee's metaphor – exactly
right, as he so often is – she was 'the tranquil night-light of our fears.'
But Marjorie was not without skill or spirit. She was highly accomplished with her needle, worked in a milliner's shop, produced very
inventive clothes from unlikely materials, and fancy-dressed the
whole family for Peace Day, where she appeared, 'tender and proud',
as Queen Elizabeth the First.

She has the mixture of excited giggling and shock mentioned
earlier when the soldier appears, or when dealing with Uncle Ray's
flattery and flirtation, or when Jones's goat appears; but she is
tomboy enough to deliver a hefty kick (though dressed in her finery)

to Granny Trill's door when knocking fails to rouse the old lady. She is as ready as the others to listen to gossip from Fred Bates or Dorothy, through she is more readily scandalised than her sister, being more retiring and reticent. Marjorie is the first of the girls to bring home a boy, Maurice, and when with him she shows shyness, softness, love and embarrassment. The essence of Marjorie is her warmth, her calmness, her beauty in its widest sense.

Dorothy

In contrast, Dorothy is a livewire of a girl, though she and Marjorie share a natural and close intimacy; indeed one of our first pictures of her shows her to be deceptively like Marjorie, as, 'slow and sleepy, the light came through her nightdress like sand through a sieve'; she was 'yawning wide, and white feathers floated out of her hair.' Even here, however, there is perhaps an underlying sexuality in the picture which is more appropriate to Dorothy than to Marjorie. For Dorothy is fireworks, gunpowder, dynamite – a less 'solid' figure than Marjorie, a quicksilver creature, daring, adventurous, exciting. When the war ends, it is Dorothy who says, 'Let's go out and see what's happening'; when Marjorie thinks it is time to go back home, it is Dorothy who wants to 'stop a minute longer . . . It wouldn't do no 'arm'; she delights in scandal and gossip, leading the girls in urging Fred Bates to tell the story of Miss Flynn; she rides a bike, she whistles; she is perhaps the only one of the three who could be bored at home (fortunately so, for her boredom saved Laurie's life when he was almost buried without having died first!)

She was the most 'physical' of the girls, despite her wispiness; her boyfriend, Leslie, was 'a shy local scoutmaster, at least until he met her'! Jones's goat holds an even greater fascination for her than for the others, with its shameless virility. Dorothy seems to feel that life is outside, waiting to be enjoyed, and she is desperate to be part of it. But – and this is very important – Dorothy could also be 'something else: a fairy-tale girl, blue as a plum, tender and sentimental.' Dorothy is the link with the outside world; she brings its activities into the Lee kitchen with her chatter, her gossip, her rumours, her tales of scandal. She also brings treats home for the children – liquorice, for instance; and Laurie clearly includes her when he describes his sisters as 'the good fortune of our lives'. Perhaps he has her particularly in mind when he refers to them collectively as 'generous, indulgent, warm-blooded, and dotty'.

Yet she remains her own woman; she seems to have an inner life which excludes the family. Two pictures in particular suggest this:

first, when all the family, of an evening, are absorbed with themselves or each other, or a fantasy, in the kitchen, Dorothy is writing a love-letter; second is the arresting picture of her in fancy dress as 'Night': 'familiar Dorothy had grown far and disturbing.'

Phyllis

Phyllis is the most enigmatic of the three girls. Laurie Lee frequently speaks in this book of being haunted by a particular memory or image; equally haunting, in its way, is an adjective he uses to describe this sister – 'sad' Phyllis. It is a somewhat puzzling word yet at the same time seems to capture her essence.

She was the youngest of the three, and as the others were closer in age she was the odd one out. Lee himself tells us this, but it is evident enough as one reads the book. Phyllis is not, of course, deliberately left out or ignored by the other two; but in the rapidly growing-up world of childhood and adolescence it was perhaps inevitable that she should always be a step or two behind Marjorie and Dorothy. She tended, therefore, to be often alone, working out her own salvation, uncomplaining, overshadowed. Her doing the mundane household chores fits in well with one's picture of Phyllis, and it is not surprising to see her, at the age of seven or eight, 'peeling spuds'; when all are gathered in the kitchen in the evening, pursuing their own interests, Phyllis is cleaning the cutlery.

It would be a great mistake, however, to think of her as some kind of household drudge: in the first place, the family did not treat her as such; in the second place, she brought a simple dignity to the most menial tasks; and thirdly, there was another side to Phyllis, a depth of introspection which, no doubt, her solitary hours had fostered. This was best seen when she was performing her favourite task, putting the young ones to bed. Young as she was, she became mature then, 'old-fashioned', with a religious earnestness; what she perhaps failed to find through companionship with her sisters she found in her motherly, guardian angel role with her young half-brothers. It is perhaps her unconscious yearning for the 'happy Eden' of the hymns she tunelessly sang that inspired the use of the word 'sad' to describe her. Many families contain a member who is referred to often with a sigh, as 'poor' – 'poor Jim', 'poor Jane', and so on; it is often very difficult to decide why they are so described – it certainly has nothing to do necessarily with money or illness; yet this is the same kind of feeling as Lee has for Phyllis: a sympathy called up by something in the very spirit of the person.

Nevertheless, by the end of *Cider with Rosie*, Phyllis (like the others) is on the verge of marriage, to Harold the Bootmaker (so designated to distinguish him from the other Harold) a serious-minded, old-fashioned boy – exactly the type one would have chosen for her. These, then, are Laurie's sisters; all of them he 'cherished', and each in her own way was for him a model of 'all that women should be in beauty, style and artifice.'

4.3.iii His brothers

Laurie's brothers appear to play a much less significant role in the book than his sisters, and it is perhaps worthwhile to pause briefly over this, and ask why. He comments at one early point that he and his brothers had never known a father's authority; it was inevitable that the strong formative influences on his early life should have been female. Remember, too, that the three girls were appreciably older than he was. In his childhood it was as if he had four mothers, but no father, or even father-figure. In the circumstances, it is hardly surprising that we hear much of Marg, Doth and Phyl, but comparatively little of the boys.

Yet although their names occur only infrequently, the reason is partly caused by Lee's use of the pronoun 'we' to mean 'we boys' – especially 'Jack and I'. Consider the situation. The girls were much older than the boys; they were fairly soon in employment, and out all day; boyfriends soon began to feature in their lives; in the house the girls shared a bedroom and many household chores. Jack, Lol and Tony were close in age: only four years separated Jack and Tony, with Lol in the middle; they too soon had 'the boys' room'; they shared their schooldays, and the many long days when the girls were at work.

In the light of this, there are surely many shared experiences with his brothers in the book which we may be inclined to overlook. Without going into detail, two sections could be specifically cited: 'Winter and Summer', in which he constantly describes what 'we' did, though rarely says who 'we' are; his brothers were with him on the carol-singing venture, however, and probably on most of the others, which after all do cover the whole year's span; and secondly 'Outings and Festivals', where again he appears to be with Jack, and probably Tony, much of the time. In brief, the natural intimacy of brothers, close in age, in that household, perhaps seems to Laurie Lee so normal and all-pervasive that it hardly needs to be spelled out.

It is time to look more closely at these brothers, with first a quick glance at the two half-brothers. *Reggie* is easily dealt with; for reasons unspecified he lived with his grandmother (his father's mother) and does not feature further in *Cider with Rosie*. *Harold*, too, figures rarely; he was younger than his sisters, but seemed much older. A practical boy, forever tinkering with bikes and engines, he presented a serious lonely front to the world, rarely sharing family laughter. Indeed, though Lee refers both to Phyllis and to Tony as the odd ones out in the family, a strong case could be made out for Harold as the most apart of them all, belonging to neither of the natural groups within the family because of his age on the one hand and his sex on the other. Alone of the children he is described as loving 'our absent father'; in which case it is little wonder that he was unhappy 'more often than not'.

Jack

Jack was the closest to Laurie of all the brothers. He was academically the brightest of the family and it is to this ability that Lee constantly returns. When we are given our first clear picture of Jack, he is the 'Infant Freak' of the village school, set apart from the other children by his quick mind and lively intelligence. He was given privileges, being upgraded to the 'Big Room' at an abnormally early age, and simply allowed (it would seem) to pursue his own studies independently of the other children, and even of his teachers. This first picture of Jack is matched by the last. On the book's final page, Jack is at the Grammar School, and doing very well. In between, too, he is presented always as alert, curious and sharp. First thing in the morning he is quizzing Laurie with titbits of general knowledge; last thing at night he is still at it when, wakened by Laurie's late arrival in bed, he asks him to 'think of a number'. At other times, he does his 'inscrutable' homework.

Though Jack was not above using his sharpness in self-interest (managing to be given more food than the others by eating 'against time' – a splendid phrase; or anticipating when there were unpleasant tasks to be done and disappearing in advance, well earning his nickname, 'the Slider') nevertheless the others seem to have admired rather than resented his craftiness. Laurie and he fought, as brothers often do; but between them they forged a relationship which excluded the rest of humanity, building – in Lee's words – 'a private structure around us'. They shared the same room, the same bed, until Laurie left home. So much were they mentally at one that Laurie felt no need in writing of those days to outline Jack's role on every occasion: he was simply there.

Tony

Tony is perhaps the most intriguing member of the whole family. As we have just seen, Lee regards him as the odd one out, not just of the boys but of the whole seven. His character is a very unusual mixture: he inspires fond affection in his sisters (as the family baby, possibly) yet has a quick tongue; he is often to be seen in a world of his own, playing solitary games made up by his fanciful imagination; yet he clearly was not the easiest of children to handle at school, being at times cheeky, defiant and stubborn. The impression is given that even the author does not feel he understands Tony fully, yet sees in him an unusual, even remarkable, human being. He calls him 'the one true visionary amongst us', an intriguing description, prompting the question: 'In what way a visionary?'

Tony was not just 'solitary'; he was '*a* solitary', and there is a great, though subtle, difference between them. Not only circumstances but also temperament are involved. Tony had a knowledge of worlds other than ours, a spiritual dimension which marked him off; his mind and body did not always seem to be interconnected: at times he seemed unhuman, in the way an insect is, or even a saint. (Lee makes both comparisons himself, of course.) When Lee thinks of him and writes of him, such words seem to occur naturally to him, as do 'hermit', 'waif', 'strange', 'brooding', 'knowing', 'deep.

Tony had a very powerful inner life, as most of these words indicate; his mind was peopled by 'secret friends' and he had appalling nightmares. His face was 'crooked' and 'suffering' (startling words to apply to a young child) yet sometimes lit up brightly from within. Significantly, he 'drew like an artist' – as if words as a medium were inadequate to give life to the vivid pictures which seared his brain. Tony, like Phyllis, but even more intensely, is a sad – even tragic – figure.

4.3.iv His mother

In the section 'Mother' we saw the influence of Mrs Lee on Laurie's development as a man and as a writer. What, however, of the essence of the woman? This is difficult to capture, for Mother Lee has the elusive quality of an exotic fragrance, or of a cake of soap in bath water.

The best starting-point is perhaps Lee's description of her (one of many) on p.126: 'she loved this world and saw it fresh with hopes that never clouded.' This certainly goes a long way towards explaining many facets of her character. That she had had a very hard life there is no doubt: a childhood in poor circumstances, a girlhood of servitude, a brief marriage, and then seven children to raise – not counting the heart-breaking death of Frances. Yet despite all this she was a 'light-giver'. In practical terms, how does her view of the world show itself?

First, it appears in her love of Nature. This goes much deeper than the rather sentimental love of flowers which characterises many human beings. It was rather a reverence for the life-force itself, and an intuitive understanding of the created world. 'Gardening' for Mrs Lee was not synonymous with 'weeding', 'tidying', and so on; she allowed everything to grow in profusion, including the weeds, to the bewilderment of birds, bees, and probably any passers-by. Every foot of earth was used, without order; though her methods were slapdash, the green life responded, overflowing in richness. Nor was it only her garden which teemed with surging vigour: the interior of the cottage too was a constant riot of growth as the garden spilled over.

The freshness of her view of the world is seen in her childlike qualities of innocence and naivety. Lee tells us that at times his mother could drive the family to distraction and shatter their nerves, yet her enthusiasm, her positive hope, her sheer joy were such that impatience with her could never turn to anger. One thinks of her setting out with the whole family, plus boy-friends, on a picnic, for instance. It is clear to the reader that the event is little short of a disaster, and the mood of the older children close to rebellion, yet Mrs Lee can gaily sail on, full of chatter, vivacious, uplifting. Or again, one thinks of her failing to realise that the new buses cannot be kept waiting as the old carrier's cart could, and blithely starting to get ready for her outing only when she hears the bus hooting a short way off. In anyone else, her unconcern would be seen as a lack of consideration, but with Mother Lee it is part and parcel of her childlike temperament: those on the bus, and she, are all off on an adventure; life is wonderful – what does time matter? (Her disregard of time may seem strange until one thinks of it as childlike; it was with her, increasingly so, almost all her days, culminating in the touching picture of her never going to bed, but sitting up in her chair all night, dozing fitfully; preparing a dinner for Laurie home on leave, unaware that dawn is breaking.)

There is something childlike also in her hope, clung to for thirty-five years, that her husband would one day return to her. Very rarely do leopards change their spots; the objective outsider would see quite clearly that Mr Lee had gone for good, but Mrs Lee fed her hope until his death, which soon was followed by hers.

While much of her time was spent in reminiscence as distinct from nostalgia she nevertheless lived only for the day, again like a child, or a bird. She was a creature of the moment, natural, free, honest. For the animals of the hedgerow this is normal and fine; but the human world has, perhaps unfortunately, developed rather differently, and Annie Lee's inability to live life in the orderly, serious fashion most people do brought problems.

When it came to money, for instance, she had no method to cope with such matters as budgeting. She would buy a whole goose for their weekend – a luxury which left little money, or food, for the rest of the week; she would take the family on an expensive trip to the theatre, but have to do without coal for the whole winter. Many are the examples of a similar sort which Lee produces. But in all this it should be noticed that her extravagance is not selfish; not for her alone are the goods they can ill afford; even the bits of china she so loves are bought for their beauty, broken though they may be. Like a jackdaw she is drawn to bright objects, and like a jackdaw she hoards, in the belief (naive again, perhaps) that things will come in useful one day. And so debts piled up at times, the rent of the cottage went unpaid, the neighbours tutted, shook their heads, and no doubt felt superior.

A similar chaos was evident in her housekeeping. Laurie tells us that he had left home before he ever lived in a house where 'corners were visible' and 'the rooms were clear and carpeted'. This characteristic more than any other seems to have been responsible for causing her husband to desert her. The newspapers of twenty years littered the floor, meals were erratic, life was unplanned. Yet her unshakeable belief in 'good fortune' would seem in some way to have been justified, for they 'got by'. It would be a mistake to think, however, that Mrs Lee was totally unaware of these shortcomings – if that is what they are. She did make attempts at order, but always retreated into muddle; to make a plan was alien to her nature.

Akin to her characteristic of living for the day is the impulsiveness of her emotions – yet again, a childlike trait. She was as extravagant and profligate with her feelings as she was with her purse. At times this would show itself in panic and hysteria, as when heavy rains brought the peril of flooding to their very door; or when she had some minor accident in the kitchen and screamed in alarm. At other times, indeed almost daily, it would be seen in grief, as she wept for Frances, the only daughter she had given birth to; or, in the later stages of her near-madness, when she was 'crying for light'. Predominant among her emotions, however, was her 'indestructible gaiety', that irrational happiness which she brought to her life, and which she instilled in some at least of her children. She lavished affection and care on her family, sealing the bond of love with her sons as each in turn shared her bed; savouring each new experience the children brought her, their accomplishments and their hopes.

These aspects of her personality perhaps make Mrs Lee seem like an overgrown child – delightful, but still only a child, with a child's immaturities. Such a picture would be very incomplete, for Mrs Lee was a very real woman too. Let us then extend our view of her. First there is her 'remarkable dignity'. For me it is most evocatively seen in her occasional lone piano-playing. Lee paints a suitably melancholy background, soft and sentimental, of green yew trees filling the quiet kitchen. Into this he introduces his mother. But this is not the mother he earlier describes as having 'hair loose-tangled . . . clothes shapelessly humped around her': this is a woman in bloom, alone, beautiful; she has dressed herself in her best – her silks – and is wearing her few pieces of jewellery. In the gathering summer dusk, with the boys off to bed, she sits to play the piano; this is an act of deliberate sentiment and nostalgia, for we know of happy times she spent with her husband, playing and singing for him. It is a scene to which we cannot fail to respond emotionally, but Annie is not wallowing in self-pity; she has the calm, sad dignity of a woman who has suffered much; 'sounds of peace, yet disturbing'.

Then there is her innate simplicity. This is no doubt a quality she has brought with her from childhood into adulthood, but the child's simplicity (seen perhaps in her love of word-play and rhyming) is very different from the adult simplicity at issue here. The two stories she tells from her days in service are good examples. In one, she was spoken to with great courtesy by an Indian Prince; in the other, a battalion of soldiers saluted her as they marched by, in full regimental dress. These simple events were 'magic encounters' from her past, retold again and again to her children; they are simple highlights of a life which saw precious little of life's ceremony, except at second hand. It is precisely because she had known so much of life's hardship and service that these two moments when she was recognised as a woman, and a beautiful one, in her own right, mean so much to her, providing a simple but endless thrill.

While there is something naive in her hope that her husband would one day return to her, there is nothing juvenile in the love, devotion, patience and sacrifice of those long years of waiting. These are all profound adult qualities, given to few (perhaps a little old-fashioned according to today's values, but high on any list of qualities which raise Man above the level of the beasts of the field; and perhaps unpopular because they are difficult to acquire.)

In some ways, then, Mother Lee seems not really to have been cut out for this world; she existed in a dreamy, unpractical state, letting her mature years slip by in waiting, rarely having a total hold on reality, never mastering life's everyday situations. Yet she was a remarkable woman, full of zest and joy, consigning the mundane to its rightful place, riding in harmony with a different kind of reality: the broader, deeper reality of the natural world. It is a fitting end to her life that she 'grew into her background' like a rose going back to nature; and unutterably touching that in her final madness she should shed the years of grief and hardship and return to her youth, her innocent girlhood.

Finally, *Cider with Rosie* contains many other memorable characters who are only omitted here because of considerations of space: in particular, Laurie's uncles, the grannies in the wainscot, Miss Flynn, and the tantalising Rosie Burdock. Lee has a remarkable ability to catch the essence of a character in a few brief phrases: one example only – his Aunt Minnie (Uncle Tom's wife) is described as a 'tiny, pretty, parted-down-the-middle woman'. How much neatness, orderliness, no-nonsense firmness is conveyed by that 'parted-down -the-middle'; a bird-like daintiness, a place for everything and everything in its place! Over and over again we see Lee pierce the outer skin, looking for the heart of his characters – real people, of course, but more difficult to sum up, not less, because of that.

5 SPECIMEN PASSAGE AND COMMENTARY

It would be hard to find in *Cider with Rosie* a passage which is untypical of the whole, so consistent is it in its tone, its style, its content. The following passage was chosen almost at random. It recounts some of the impressions of summer, from the section 'Winter and Summer'; and in particular recalls visits to the Robinsons' to play with the five children in the bogland near their farm cottage.

We moved. We went to the shop and bought sherbet and sucked it through sticks of liquorice. Sucked gently, the sherbet merely dusted the tongue; too hard, and you choked with sweet powders; or if you blew back through the tube the sherbet-bag burst and you disappeared in a blizzard of sugar. Sucking and blowing, coughing and weeping, we scuffled our way down the lane. We drank at the spring to clean our mouths, then threw water at each other and made rainbows. Mr Jones's pond was bubbling with life, and covered with great white lilies – they poured from their leaves like candle-fat, ran molten, then cooled on the water. Moorhens plopped, and dabchicks scooted, insects rowed and skated. New-hatched frogs hopped about like flies, lizards gulped in the grass. The lane itself was crusted with cow-dung, hard baked and smelling good.

We met Sixpence Robinson among the bulrushes, and he said, 'Come and have some fun.' He lived along the lane just past the sheepwash in a farm cottage near a bog. There were five in his family, two girls and three boys, and their names all began with S. There was Sis and Sloppy, Stosher and Sammy, and our good friend Sixpence the Tanner. Sis and Sloppy were both beautiful girls and used to hide from us boys in the gooseberries. It was the brothers we played with: and Sammy, though a cripple, was one of the most agile lads in the village.

Theirs was a good place to be at any time, and they were good to be with. (Like us, they had no father; unlike ours, he was dead.) So today, in the spicy heat of their bog, we sat round on logs and whistled, peeled sticks, played mouth-organs, dammed up the stream, and cut harbours in the cool clay banks. Then we took all the pigeons out of their dovecots and ducked them in the water-butt, held them under till their beaks started bubbling then threw them up in the air. Splashing spray from their wings they flew round the house, then came back to roost like fools. (Sixpence had a one-eyed pigeon called Spike who he boasted could stay under longest, but one day the poor bird, having broken all records, crashed for ever among the cabbages.)

When all this was over, we retired to the paddock and played cricket under the trees. Sammy, in his leg-irons, charged up and down. Hens and guinea-fowl took to the trees. Sammy hopped and bowled like murder at us, and we defended our stumps with our lives. The cracked bat clouting; the cries in the reeds; the smells of fowls and water; the long afternoon with the steep hills around us watched by Sloppy still hid in the gooseberries – it seemed down here that no disasters could happen, that nothing could ever touch us. This was Sammy's and Sixpence's; the place past the sheepwash, the hide-out unspoiled by authority, where drowned pigeons flew and cripples ran free; where it was summer, in some ways, always.

What Lee presents here, as so often in the book, is a composite picture, an essence distilled from many similar days, possibly over a few summers. The children are seen enjoying a natural, almost naked freedom, in which they mingle with the rest of the created world; it is a picture not so much of the innocence of childhood as of its unfettered joy. In their play is no sense of past or future; the sensations of the present are all, in a timeless world of magic – 'the place past the sheepwash'. The tone is full of good humour, with perhaps a gentle yearning for those days which are lost to him for ever.

What follows now is an examination of each of the four paragraphs in turn, with aspects of the writing picked out piecemeal for comment; these comments may be related to those made elsewhere in this book on themes, style, and so on.

In the first paragraph we can observe the typical boys' activities, with sherbet and water – a mixture of mischief, experiment and delight (in the rainbowed water-drops and the varied properties of sherbet). Laurie is very much one of them – just an ordinary lad, accepted as such by the others. Notice also the figurative language: metaphor ('a blizzard of sugar'); onomatopoeia ('plopped', 'gulped'); a fine simile ('They poured from their leaves like candle-fat, ran molten, then cooled on the water'); a nicely balanced piece of phrasing ('Sucking and blowing, coughing and weeping').

Along similar lines is the interesting selection of vocabulary, especially verbs: 'dusted', 'choked', 'scuffled', 'bubbling', 'scooted', 'rowed', 'skated'. So much colour and richness is added to language when such words are used so often, and neutral, vague ones so seldom. This quality allies naturally with the richness of the sensuous experience in the paragraph; all the senses are at work here, but especially taste, with the evocation of the clean, purifying water, and the throat-catching sherbet.

Three elements might be identified in the second paragraph. First is the innocent, childish humour of the Robinson children's names all beginning with S. The young boy does not apparently realise that the names, with the exception of Sammy, are not names at all but nicknames, and probably given in any case because of their alliterative quality! This poking fun at himself for his child-like naivety is very typical of Lee, of course, as we have seen elswhere.

Second is the underlying sexuality of the Robinson girls hiding from the boys in the gooseberry bushes. The girls clearly want to be near the boys – especially the Lee boys, who are not 'family' – and yet have an instinctive shyness mingled with fear which makes them hide. (Hiding and being found figure in many children's games, of course, for a variety of psychological and other reasons; here, one feels the girls are drawn by the 'exclusive' male ritual of playing cricket, of which they wish to be hidden, yet not unseen, witnesses.)

Third is the 'fearless frankness' with which the word 'cripple' is used. It has never been Lee's way, as we have seen before, to shy away from harsh reality – quite the opposite; society all too often creates taboos: subjects which are not mentioned, or only whispered about, or given euphemisms – cancer, AIDS, and so on. Lee, typically, does not flinch from reality – a cripple is a cripple and that is the word he uses; 'physically handicapped', most would say, to blunt the sharp edge of truth, but not Lee.

A not dissimilar point may be noticed in paragraph three, when he writes of the death of the pigeon, a one-eyed creature which 'crashed for ever among the cabbages'. Here, not only is the matter of the bird's death faced head-on, but treated with a little black comedy. The tone of this third paragraph is also noteworthy. It typifies the essential good humour and friendliness of the writer; the enormous pleasure he derives from his fellows: 'Theirs was a good place to be at any time, and they were good to be with.'

Notice also the terse comment about his father: ('Like us, they had no father; unlike ours, he was dead.') In its brusqueness of tone it rings like an accusation; but written as a bracketed aside it relegates his father to the level of an irrelevance. The double-edged attitude is neatly, even brilliantly, conveyed in a sentence of less than a dozen words. Lastly there is a stylistic point: again the typical listing device, this time of activities: 'we sat round on logs and whistled, peeled sticks, played mouth-organs, dammed up the stream, and cut harbours in the cool clay banks.' The endless, meaningless, yet meaningful busy-ness of the boys is manifest.

In the final paragraph of this extract are some features already noticed, but worth pointing out again. The good humour to be seen in the image of the hens scattering in terror when the cricket begins is one example; a second is yet another list, this time an evocative piling-up of sensations in the sentence beginning, 'The cracked bat clouting' – so redolent of idle summers; and we see again the directness and frankness spotted earlier, in the image of Sammy 'in his leg-irons'.

A new note is sounded, however, in the revealing phrase, 'unspoiled by authority'; Lee's view of authority has been commented upon at length, and this is simply a further indication of his attitude: authority 'spoils'. This paragraph, indeed, is full of the unchained freedom of children at play, wild in their natural surroundings, natural in their wild environment.

Finally there is a quality at the very heart of *Cider with Rosie*: the sense of magic and wonder in the world of childhood; a world 'where drowned pigeons flew and cripples ran free; where it was summer, in some ways, always.' (Bearing in mind that Lee is writing these words in his forties, it is possible to discern a gentle nostalgia, too, for that summer world so long ago.)

6 CRITICAL RECEPTION

The popular success of *Cider with Rosie* can hardly be over-emphasised; it has been outstanding. It is worth noting, moreover, that very few writers whose work is taken seriously enough to be used for academic study have enjoyed in their own lifetime, and so soon after publication, the success of Laurie Lee.

That success was almost immediate. Within a year of its British publication, in 1959, *Cider with Rosie* was published in the United States of America, with the title: *Edge of Day: Boyhood in the West of England*. In 1962 came the first Penguin edition of the work, since when it has been reprinted at least twenty-five times by Penguin, its total sales being in the region of two millions.

As early as 1961, part of *Cider with Rosie* ('The Uncles') was selected by James Reeves to appear in his book *Great English Essays* (Published by Cassell). Lee's quality was thus instantly ranked alongside great English prose writers of the past – a fine tribute. Reeves wrote: 'This autobiography . . . recreates with passionate intensity the scenes and characters of a vanished rural order.' Another distinguished early reviewer (H. E. Bates in *The Sunday Times*) spoke of 'a prose poem that flashes and winks like a prism'. In a very different way, the instant 'classic' status of *Cider with Rosie* has been recognised by its inclusion in a delightful book called *How to Become Ridiculously Well-Read in One Evening* (published by Viking in 1985) in which V. Ernest Cox produces a brief, witty summary of the book, in verse.

Laurie Lee already had a firm reputation as a poet before the publication of *Cider with Rosie*, the eminent critic Cyril Connolly having been instrumental in getting Lee's early poems published. His poetry has not been widely anthologised, however – perhaps surprisingly – being omitted from most of the representative selections of the poetry of the 1940s and 1950s. But poetry during this century has decreased alarmingly in popular appeal, with a few notable exceptions. This, his first major prose work, brought him to the attention of a very wide audience, and a very diverse one, for much of the success of the book in terms of its huge sales must be due to its being enjoyed by people of all ages from the teens upwards, regardless of social class or background. Clearly there is an appeal to experiences common to us all at the heart of *Cider with Rosie* which, combined with its astonishing vividness of language, has given it world-wide recognition. His popular appeal has even led to his appearance on a Terry Wogan chat show – an interview in which, as he takes a certain amount of pleasure in recounting, 'We didn't hit it off at all.'

Examination Boards quickly came to see the value of *Cider with Rosie* as a set text in English Literature studies, and it has appeared very regularly on the syllabuses of all the major boards for several years. Clearly this is because of the quality of writing rather than that the book deals with the writer's childhood and adolescence, and might therefore be considered suitable for adolescent readers. For the simple fact is that the book has proved immensely popular with readers of all ages.

The success of *Cider with Rosie* ensured Lee's reputation as a supremely gifted prose writer, and his subsequent work has quickly been acclaimed; in particular the continuation of his autobiography in *As I Walked Out One Midsummer Morning*. Because Lee's writing evokes such powerful visual images it is not surprising that those who deal in visual media saw his potential for adaptation; the BBC produced in 1986 a beautifully filmed two-hour recreation of *As I Walked Out*, with Lee himself reading the extracts in his rich West Country voice.

In a fascinating interview he gave to Val Hennessy in *The Times* (18 Feb, 1986) Lee conceded: 'It's fairly true to my book – the young man taking my part is much better-looking than I was'. He also had interesting comments to make about *Cider with Rosie*: 'My serious objection to being on the syllabus is the daft exam questions they set'; and he claims to be unable to understand why a book about English rural life sixty and more years ago should be of interest to today's readers.

Of interest it remains, however; and though he had 'never intended to be a writer' there are hopes that a third autobiographical work, about the Spanish Civil War, will soon appear; he is also writing what he calls his 'Deathbed Confessions' – one hopes their title will have no literal relevance for many years to come.

REVISION QUESTIONS

1. Using Sections 1 to 3, show how Laurie Lee's horizons widened as he grew up.
2. Imagine Lee kept a diary as a child. Write the entry for a typical day in the summer holidays of 1924.
3. In what ways which affected his life was England in Lee's childhood different from now?
4. Justify, by examining many examples, Lee's statement that 'there was a frank, unfearful attitude towards death'.
5. Write character sketches of any two of 'the uncles'.
6. Describe half a dozen aspects of Mrs Lee's behaviour which might be called 'unusual'.
7. Imagine you are Mrs Lee. All the children are out or in bed. You sit musing about your your past, in front of the fire. Write your thoughts.
8. Which is your favourite episode in the book? Describe what happens, and say why you like it.
9. If you had lived in the Lee household, what would you have liked most about their life, and what least?
10. A book's title is important. Write fully about the two titles of the book: *Cider with Rosie* and *Edge of Day*.
11. Lee has called *Cider with Rosie* 'a celebration'. Discuss the appropriateness of this description of the book.

FURTHER READING

Other works by Laurie Lee

The Sun My Monument (Hogarth Press, London, 1944)
The Bloom of Candles (Lehmann, London, 1947)
The Voyage of Magellan (Lehmann, London, 1948)
My Many-Coated Man (André Deutsch, London, 1955)
A Rose for Winter (Hogarth Press, London, 1961)
The Firstborn (Hogarth Press, London, 1964)
As I Walked Out One Midsummer Morning (Penguin Books, Harmondsworth, 1969)
I Can't Stay Long (Penguin Books, Harmondsworth 1975)

Useful Comparative work
Collected Poems of Dylan Thomas (J. M. Dent, 1952) in particular 'Fern Hill' and 'Poem in October'
Under Milk Wood by Dylan Thomas (J. M. Dent, London 1954)
Miscellany One by Dylan Thomas (J. M. Dent, London 1963)
Songs of Innocence by William Blake. (See Alan Tomlinson's Master Guide in this series.)

Mastering English Literature

Richard Gill

Mastering English Literature will help readers both to enjoy English Literature and to be successful in 'O' levels, 'A' levels and other public exams. It is an introduction to the study of poetry, novels and drama which helps the reader in four ways – by providing ways of approaching literature, by giving examples and practice exercises, by offering hints on how to write about literature, and by the author's own evident enthusiasm for the subject. With extracts from more than 200 texts, this is an enjoyable account of how to get the maximum satisfaction out of reading, whether it be for formal examinations or simply for pleasure.

Work Out English Literature ('A' level)

S.H. Burton

This book familiarises 'A' level English Literature candidates with every kind of test which they are likely to encounter. Suggested answers are worked out step by step and accompanied by full author's commentary. The book helps students to clarify their aims and establish techniques and standards so that they can make appropriate responses to similar questions when the examination pressures are on. It opens up fresh ways of looking at the full range of set texts, authors and critical judgements and motivates students to know more of these matters.

Also from Macmillan

CASEBOOK SERIES

The Macmillan *Casebook* series brings together the best of modern criticism with a selection of early reviews and comments. Each Casebook charts the development of opinion on a play, poem, or novel, or on a literary genre, from its first appearance to the present day.

GENERAL THEMES

COMEDY: DEVELOPMENTS IN
CRITICISM
D. J. Palmer

DRAMA CRITICISM:
DEVELOPMENTS SINCE IBSEN
A. J. Hinchliffe

THE ENGLISH NOVEL:
DEVELOPMENTS IN CRITICISM
SINCE HENRY JAMES
Stephen Hazell

THE LANGUAGE OF LITERATURE
N. Page

THE PASTORAL MODE
Bryan Loughrey

THE ROMANTIC IMAGINATION
J. S. Hill

TRAGEDY: DEVELOPMENTS IN
CRITICISM
R. P. Draper

POETRY

WILLIAM BLAKE: SONGS OF
INNOCENCE AND EXPERIENCE
Margaret Bottrall

BROWNING: MEN AND WOMEN
AND OTHER POEMS
J. R. Watson

BYRON: CHILDE HAROLD'S
PILGRIMAGE AND DON JUAN
John Jump

CHAUCER: THE CANTERBURY
TALES
J. J. Anderson

COLERIDGE: THE ANCIENT
MARINER AND OTHER POEMS
A. R. Jones and W. Tydeman

DONNE: SONGS AND SONETS
Julian Lovelock

T. S. ELIOT: FOUR QUARTETS
Bernard Bergonzi

T. S. ELIOT: PRUFROCK,
GERONTION, ASH WEDNESDAY
AND OTHER POEMS
B. C. Southam

T. S. ELIOT: THE WASTELAND
C. B. Cox and A. J. Hinchliffe

ELIZABETHAN POETRY: LYRICAL
AND NARRATIVE
Gerald Hammond

THOMAS HARDY: POEMS
J. Gibson and T. Johnson

GERALD MANLEY HOPKINS:
POEMS
Margaret Bottrall

KEATS: ODES
G. S. Fraser

KEATS: THE NARRATIVE POEMS
J. S. Hill

MARVELL: POEMS
Arthur Pollard

THE METAPHYSICAL POETS
Gerald Hammond

MILTON: PARADISE LOST
A. E. Dyson and Julian Lovelock

POETRY OF THE FIRST WORLD
WAR
Dominic Hibberd

ALEXANDER POPE: THE RAPE OF
THE LOCK
John Dixon Hunt

SHELLEY: SHORTER POEMS &
LYRICS
Patrick Swinden

SPENSER: THE FAERIE QUEEN
Peter Bayley

TENNYSON: IN MEMORIAM
John Dixon Hunt

THIRTIES POETS: 'THE AUDEN
GROUP'
Ronald Carter

WORDSWORTH: LYRICAL
BALLADS
A. R. Jones and W. Tydeman

WORDSWORTH: THE PRELUDE
W. J. Harvey and R. Gravil

W. B. YEATS: POEMS 1919–1935
E. Cullingford

W. B. YEATS: LAST POEMS
Jon Stallworthy

THE NOVEL AND PROSE

JANE AUSTEN: EMMA
David Lodge

JANE AUSTEN: NORTHANGER
ABBEY AND PERSUASION
B. C. Southam

JANE AUSTEN: SENSE AND
SENSIBILITY, PRIDE AND
PREJUDICE AND MANSFIELD
PARK
B. C. Southam

CHARLOTTE BRONTË: JANE EYRE
AND VILLETTE
Miriam Allott

EMILY BRONTË: WUTHERING
HEIGHTS
Miriam Allott

BUNYAN: THE PILGRIM'S
PROGRESS
R. Sharrock

CONRAD: HEART OF DARKNESS,
NOSTROMO AND UNDER
WESTERN EYES
C. B. Cox

CONRAD: THE SECRET AGENT
Ian Watt

CHARLES DICKENS: BLEAK
HOUSE
A. E. Dyson

CHARLES DICKENS: DOMBEY
AND SON AND LITTLE DORRITT
Alan Shelston

CHARLES DICKENS: HARD TIMES,
GREAT EXPECTATIONS AND OUR
MUTUAL FRIEND
N. Page

GEORGE ELIOT: MIDDLEMARCH
Patrick Swinden

GEORGE ELIOT: THE MILL ON
THE FLOSS AND SILAS MARNER
R. P. Draper

HENRY FIELDING: TOM JONES
Neil Compton

E. M. FORSTER: A PASSAGE TO
INDIA
Malcolm Bradbury

HARDY: THE TRAGIC NOVELS
R. P. Draper

HENRY JAMES: WASHINGTON
SQUARE AND THE PORTRAIT OF
A LADY
Alan Shelston

JAMES JOYCE: DUBLINERS AND A
PORTRAIT OF THE ARTIST AS A
YOUNG MAN
Morris Beja

D. H. LAWRENCE: THE RAINBOW
AND WOMEN IN LOVE
Colin Clarke

D. H. LAWRENCE: SONS AND
LOVERS
Gamini Salgado

SWIFT: GULLIVER'S TRAVELS
Richard Gravil

THACKERAY: VANITY FAIR
Arthur Pollard

TROLLOPE: THE BARSETSHIRE
NOVELS
T. Bareham

VIRGINIA WOOLF: TO THE
LIGHTHOUSE
Morris Beja

DRAMA

CONGREVE: COMEDIES
Patrick Lyons

T. S. ELIOT: PLAYS
Arnold P. Hinchliffe

JONSON: EVERY MAN IN HIS
HUMOUR AND THE ALCHEMIST
R. V. Holdsworth

JONSON: VOLPONE
J. A. Barish

MARLOWE: DR FAUSTUS
John Jump

MARLOWE: TAMBURLAINE,
EDWARD II AND THE JEW OF
MALTA
John Russell Brown

MEDIEVAL ENGLISH DRAMA
Peter Happé

O'CASEY: JUNO AND THE
PAYCOCK, THE PLOUGH AND THE
STARS AND THE SHADOW OF A
GUNMAN
R. Ayling

JOHN OSBORNE: LOOK BACK IN
ANGER
John Russell Taylor

WEBSTER: THE WHITE DEVIL AND
THE DUCHESS OF MALFI
R. V. Holdsworth

WILDE: COMEDIES
W. Tydeman

SHAKESPEARE

SHAKESPEARE: ANTONY AND
CLEOPATRA
John Russell Brown

SHAKESPEARE: CORIOLANUS
B. A. Brockman

SHAKESPEARE: HAMLET
John Jump

SHAKESPEARE: HENRY IV PARTS
I AND II
G. K. Hunter

SHAKESPEARE: HENRY V
Michael Quinn

SHAKESPEARE: JULIUS CAESAR
Peter Ure

SHAKESPEARE: KING LEAR
Frank Kermode

SHAKESPEARE: MACBETH
John Wain

SHAKESPEARE: MEASURE FOR
MEASURE
G. K. Stead

SHAKESPEARE: THE MERCHANT
OF VENICE
John Wilders

SHAKESPEARE: A MIDSUMMER
NIGHT'S DREAM
A. W. Price

SHAKESPEARE: MUCH ADO
ABOUT NOTHING AND AS YOU
LIKE IT
John Russell Brown

SHAKESPEARE: OTHELLO
John Wain

SHAKESPEARE: RICHARD II
N. Brooke

SHAKESPEARE: THE SONNETS
Peter Jones

SHAKESPEARE: THE TEMPEST
D. J. Palmer

SHAKESPEARE: TROILUS AND
CRESSIDA
Priscilla Martin

SHAKESPEARE: TWELFTH NIGHT
D. J. Palmer

SHAKESPEARE: THE WINTER'S
TALE
Kenneth Muir

MACMILLAN SHAKESPEARE VIDEO WORKSHOPS

DAVID WHITWORTH

Three unique book and video packages, each examining a particular aspect of Shakespeare's work; tragedy, comedy and the Roman plays. Designed for all students of Shakespeare, each package assumes no previous knowledge of the plays and can serve as a useful introduction to Shakespeare for 'O' and 'A' level candidates as well as for students at colleges and institutes of further, higher and adult education.

The material is based on the New Shakespeare Company Workshops at the Roundhouse, adapted and extended for television. By combining the resources of television and a small theatre company, this exploration of Shakespeare's plays offers insights into varied interpretations, presentation, styles of acting as well as useful background information.

While being no substitute for seeing the whole plays in performance, it is envisaged that these video cassettes will impart something of the original excitement of the theatrical experience, and serve as a welcome complement to textual analysis leading to an enriched and broader view of the plays.

Each package consists of:

* the Macmillan Shakespeare editions of the plays concerned;
* a video cassette available in VHS or Beta;
* a leaflet of teacher's notes.

THE TORTURED MIND
looks at the four tragedies Hamlet, Othello, Macbeth and King Lear.

THE COMIC SPIRIT
examines the comedies Much Ado About Nothing, Twelfth Night, A Midsummer Night's Dream, and As You Like It.

THE ROMAN PLAYS
Features Julius Caesar, Antony and Cleopatra and Coriolanus

THE MACMILLAN SHAKESPEARE

General Editor: PETER HOLLINDALE
Advisory Editor: PHILIP BROCKBANK

The Macmillan Shakespeare features:
* clear and uncluttered texts with modernised punctuation and spelling wherever possible;
* full explanatory notes printed on the page facing the relevant text for ease of reference;
* stimulating introductions which concentrate on content, dramatic effect, character and imagery, rather than mere dates and sources.

Above all, The Macmillan Shakespeare treats each play as a work for the theatre which can also be enjoyed on the page.

CORIOLANUS
Editor: Tony Parr

THE WINTER'S TALE
Editor: Christopher Parry

MUCH ADO ABOUT NOTHING
Editor: Jan McKeith

RICHARD II
Editor: Richard Adams

RICHARD III
Editor: Richard Adams

HENRY IV, PART I
Editor: Peter Hollindale

HENRY IV, PART II
Editor: Tony Parr

HENRY V
Editor: Brian Phythian

AS YOU LIKE IT
Editor: Peter Hollindale

A MIDSUMMER NIGHT'S DREAM
Editor: Norman Sanders

THE MERCHANT OF VENICE
Editor: Christopher Parry

THE TAMING OF THE SHREW
Editor: Robin Hood

TWELFTH NIGHT
Editor: E. A. J. Honigmann

THE TEMPEST
Editor: A. C. Spearing

ROMEO AND JULIET
Editor: James Gibson

JULIUS CAESAR
Editor: D. R. Elloway

MACBETH
Editor: D. R. Elloway

HAMLET
Editor: Nigel Alexander

ANTONY AND CLEOPATRA
Editors: Jan McKeith and
Richard Adams

OTHELLO
Editors: Celia Hilton and R. T. Jones

KING LEAR
Editor: Philip Edwards

MACMILLAN STUDENTS' NOVELS

General Editor: JAMES GIBSON

The Macmillan Students' Novels are low-priced, new editions of major classics, aimed at the first examination candidate. Each volume contains:

* enough explanation and background material to make the novels accessible — and rewarding — to pupils with little or no previous knowledge of the author or the literary period;

* detailed notes elucidate matters of vocabulary, interpretation and historical background;

* eight pages of plates comprising facsimiles of manuscripts and early editions, portraits of the author and photographs of the geographical setting of the novels.

JANE AUSTEN: MANSFIELD PARK
Editor: Richard Wirdnam

JANE AUSTEN: NORTHANGER ABBEY
Editor: Raymond Wilson

JANE AUSTEN: PRIDE AND PREJUDICE
Editor: Raymond Wilson

JANE AUSTEN: SENSE AND SENSIBILITY
Editor: Raymond Wilson

JANE AUSTEN: PERSUASION
Editor: Richard Wirdnam

CHARLOTTE BRONTË: JANE EYRE
Editor: F. B. Pinion

EMILY BRONTË: WUTHERING HEIGHTS
Editor: Graham Handley

JOSEPH CONRAD: LORD JIM
Editor: Peter Hollindale

CHARLES DICKENS: GREAT EXPECTATIONS
Editor: James Gibson

CHARLES DICKENS: HARD TIMES
Editor: James Gibson

CHARLES DICKENS: OLIVER TWIST
Editor: Guy Williams

CHARLES DICKENS: A TALE OF TWO CITIES
Editor: James Gibson

GEORGE ELIOT: SILAS MARNER
Editor: Norman Howlings

GEORGE ELIOT: THE MILL ON THE FLOSS
Editor: Graham Handley

D. H. LAWRENCE: SONS AND LOVERS
Editor: James Gibson

D. H. LAWRENCE: THE RAINBOW
Editor: James Gibson

MARK TWAIN: HUCKLEBERRY FINN
Editor: Christopher Parry